The Politics
of the
Equal Rights
Amendment

Conflict and the Decision Process

Janet K. Boles
The University of Texas at Austin

Longman
New York and London

For Frank and Christine

THE POLITICS OF THE EQUAL RIGHTS AMENDMENT
Conflict and the Decision Process

Longman Inc., New York
Associated companies, branches, and representatives throughout the world.

Copyright © 1979 by Longman Inc.

Developmental Editor: Nicole Benevento
Editorial and Design Supervisor: Linda Salmonson
Design: Patricia Smythe
Manufacturing and Production Supervisor: Louis Gaber
Composition: A & S Graphics, Inc.
Printing and Binding: Fairfield Graphics

Library of Congress Cataloging in Publication Data
Boles, Janet K. 1944–
    The Politics of the equal rights amendment.

    Bibliography: p.
    Includes index.
    1. Equal Rights Amendment Project.   2. Women—Legal
status, laws, etc.—United States.   3. Sex
discrimination against women—
Law and legislation—United States.   I. Title.
HQ1426.B68   342′.73′087   78-11052
ISBN 0-582-28090-7 pbk.

Manufactured in the United States of America

Contents

3 The Group Basis of Conflict   61

4 The Lobbying Campaign   100

List of Tables

List of Figures

Preface

From November 18 through 21, 1977, the federally funded National Women's Conference was held in Houston, Texas. At this conference and at the 56 State/Territorial meetings preceding it, one issue dominated the proceedings: the ratification of a proposed Constitutional amendment (popularly called the "Equal Rights Amendment") which would remove gender as a factor in establishing the legal rights of men and women. Repeatedly at the conference, the chant "E-R-A, E-R-A" rang out from amendment supporters. Across town, amendment opponents held a counterrally, billed as "Pro-Family," a term which had become a codeword for opposition to the ERA. As a further indicator of the importance this conflict had assumed in American politics, a major television network earlier in the year had presented a special report entitled "ERA: The War Between the Women."

This is not, however, a book on the Equal Rights Amendment per se. It is a study of political decision making under conditions of high conflict. It traces the ERA from its original appearance on the political agenda to the resolution of the issue through authoritative decision making. The theoretical focus is upon a synthesis of the models associated with traditional interest group politics and community conflict within the context of American state politics.

This analysis is based primarily on research done during a four-month period, January–May 1974, in three states: Texas, Georgia, and Illinois. To supplement these case studies, one week was spent in Washington, D.C., in December 1974, in interviews with those active at the national level in ERA ratification. A newspaper clipping service was also used to follow the progress of the ERA in all states, 1972 to date.

I am not neutral on the issue of the Equal Rights Amendment. I was a feminist when I began planning this project in the summer of 1973, and I became even more active in the women's movement while actually doing the research. Although I personally support the ratification of the ERA and reject most of the arguments against it advanced by its opponents, I do not expect that my analysis and interpretation will please partisans on either side. The dispassionate analytical language of the social scientist may seem obscene to those who care so deeply about the amendment's ultimate fate. To those people I can say only that, though personally not neutral, I did attempt to be fair to both sides.

Robert L. Lineberry of Northwestern University and Lawrence C. Dodd of the University of Texas at Austin read and commented on various versions of the manuscript and offered valuable suggestions. The Washington, D.C., staffs of the League of Women Voters, National Organization for Women, National Federation of Business and Professional Women's Clubs, National Women's Political Caucus, Common Cause, and the American Association of University Women generously shared data and materials. I particularly want to thank staff members Barbara Burton, Elizabeth Cox, Carol Dana, Diane Saulter, and Judith Wiebe Stafford. A grant from the National Science Foundation provided funds to cover research expenses.

I am very much indebted to all these people and organizations for their assistance and cooperation. My greatest debt, however, is to those 78 men and women in Texas, Georgia, and Illinois who, through their participation in formal interviews, helped me to understand what happened to the Equal Rights Amendment in these states.

1 Conflict and the Equal Rights Amendment

On March 22, 1972, almost 50 years after its initial introduction, a proposed amendment to the Constitution of the United States providing that "equality of rights under the law shall not be denied or abridged by the United States or any State on account of sex" was sent by the Congress to the states for ratification. The basic principle on which the amendment rests is that gender should not be a factor in determining the legal rights of either men or women. As interpreted by its supporters in Congress, the amendment was to eliminate those forms of sex discrimination that emanate from administrative, statutory, and constitutional law; governmental action; and those private sector actions that are subject to public regulation. The amendment would be tangible evidence that all governments—federal, state, and local—are committed to equal treatment under law.

This Equal Rights Amendment (ERA) received overwhelming support in both houses of Congress, passing by a vote of 354 to 23 in the House and 84 to 8 in the Senate. Both major political parties had repeatedly supported the ERA in their national party platforms, and, in 1972, reiterated their support. The previous six Presidents (and now President and Mrs. Carter) had endorsed the amendment. A lengthy and impressive list of national associations and interest groups, including, with few exceptions, every major women's organization, was on record in support of the ERA. These included such groups as the American Association of University Women, the General Federation of Women's Clubs, the National Organization for Women, the National Federation of Business and Professional Women's Clubs, Common Cause, and the American Civil Liberties Union. Moreover, a number of distinguished constitutional scholars had testified before Congress urging passage of the ERA.The American Bar Association also had adopted a resolution of endorsement. Finally, awareness of the pervasiveness of sex discrimination in society was widespread, as evidenced in public opinion surveys, and the climate of opinion for the elimination of these legal barriers to sexual equality was increasingly supportive.

TABLE 1.1
Ratification of the Equal Rights Amendment, 1972–78

State	Date	House Vote	Senate Vote
Hawaii	22 March 1972	51–0	25–0
Delaware	23 March 1972	37–0	16–0
Nebraska[1]	23 March 1972		38–0
New Hampshire	23 March 1972	179–81	21–0
Idaho[2]	24 March 1972	59–5	31–4
Iowa	24 March 1972	73–14	44–1
Kansas	28 March 1972	86–37	34–5
Texas	30 March 1972	133–9	Voice Vote
Maryland	4 April 1972	86–32	43–0
Tennessee[3]	4 April 1972	70–0	25–5
Alaska	5 April 1972	38–2	16–2
Rhode Island	14 April 1972	70–12	39–11
New Jersey	17 April 1972	62–4	34–0
Wisconsin	20 April 1972	81–11	29–4
W. Virginia	22 April 1972	Unrecorded	31–0
Colorado	24 April 1972	61–0	30–1
New York	3 May 1972	117–25	51–4
Michigan	22 May 1972	90–18	Voice Vote
Kentucky[4]	15 June 1972	56–31	20–18
Massachusetts	21 June 1972	205–7	Voice Vote
Pennsylvania	20 September 1972	178–3	43–3
California	13 November 1972	54–16	29–9

TABLE 1.1
Ratification of the Equal Rights Amendment, 1972–78 (*Cont.*)

State	Date	House Vote	Senate Vote
Wyoming	24 January 1973	40–21	17–12
South Dakota	2 February 1973	43–27	22–13
Minnesota	8 February 1973	104–28	48–18
Oregon	8 February 1973	50–9	23–6
New Mexico	13 February 1973	40–22	33–8
Vermont	21 February 1973	120–28	19–8
Connecticut	15 March 1973	99–47	27–9
Washington	22 March 1973	78–19	29–19
Maine	18 January 1974	76–68	19–11
Montana	21 January 1974	73–23	28–22
Ohio	7 February 1974	54–40	20–12
North Dakota	3 February 1975	51–49	28–22
Indiana	18 January 1977	54–45	26–24

[1]Rescinded in 1973, 31–17.
[2]Rescinded in 1977, 44–26 (House) and 16–15 (Senate).
[3]Rescinded in 1974, 56–33 (House) and 17–11 (Senate).
[4]Rescinded in 1978, 61–28 (House) and 23–15 (Senate). Vetoed by acting governor.

States unratified: Alabama, Arizona, Arkansas, Florida, Georgia, Illinois, Louisiana, Mississippi, Missouri, Nevada, North Carolina, Oklahoma, South Carolina, Utah, Virginia.

In view of this broad base of political, public, and legal opinion in favor of the ERA, political observers expected that it would be ratified by the required 38 states long before the deadline of March 22, 1979, set by Congress in the joint resolution proposing the amendment. And, indeed, in 1972, 22 state legislatures did approve the ERA. Since that time, however, its momentum sharply decreased. By November 1978, only 13 additional states had ratified and 4 states had voted to rescind their earlier approval. (See table 1.1 for a list of ratifying states.) Though it remains unclear whether a state has the power under the Constitution to rescind its ratification of a proposed amendment, the political importance of such an action cannot be dismissed. Why *did* the ERA, seemingly supported by the traditional political bases of power, encounter such strong opposition in many state legislatures? Untangling this mystery is the main purpose of this study.

While the amendment was before Congress in 1970–1972, vigorous antagonism was rarely expressed by any faction outside that small group within Congress voting against final passage. Lobbying for the ERA was heavy and well-organized, but no countervailing force was ever mobilized in any effective way. Formally in opposition were (or soon would be) groups such as the American Party, the National States' Rights Party, the National Council of Catholic Women, the John Birch Society, the Daughters of the American Revolution, and numerous ad hoc groups, primarily Stop ERA and Happiness of Womanhood (HOW). No organization in this group has a national reputation for political effectiveness and many, because of their far-right political orientation, have very negative public reputations.

With the submission of the ERA to the states, however, members of opposition groups, still far outflanked in terms of total numerical strength, were able to articulate an extremely damaging interpretation of the impact of this Amendment. According to opponents, women would not only be subject to the military draft but also assigned to combat duty. Full-time housewives and mothers would be forced to join the labor force in order to provide one-half the financial support of the family. Furthermore, women would no longer enjoy existing advantages under state domestic relations codes and under labor law.

The 1972 Platform of the American Party, the third party, which nominated Alabama Governor George Wallace for president in 1968, echoed a theme that was to become common in the ensuing debate: the threat this amendment poses to the home, the family, and American democracy and its close association with the new feminist movement:

> This deceit is planned to "liberate" women from their families, homes, and property, and as in Communist countries, they would share hard labor alongside men. Women of the American Party say "NO" to this insidious socialist plan to destroy the home, make women slaves of the government, and their children wards of the state. We urge the people to notify their state legislators to resist adoption of the so-called "Equal Rights Amendment" commonly known as "Women's Lib."

The John Birch Society, too, saw in the ERA "the Communist plans and purposes at work in a now vast effort to reduce human beings to living at the same level as animals."[1] Dr. Jonathan H. Pincus, Professor of Neurology at the Yale Medical School, in an equally dire prediction, stated that the ERA "would bring social disruption, unhappiness, and increasing rates of divorce and desertion. Weakening of family ties may also lead to increased rates of alcoholism, suicide, and possibly sexual deviation."[2] Jaquie Davison, President of Happiness of Womanhood, warned state legislators in her testimony at open hearings that "with the ERA homosexuals and lesbians would be allowed to marry. Will they next demand the privilege to adopt children?"

Once it became apparent that this interpretation of the amendment posed a threat to state ratification, proponents, no less than opponents, were willing to reduce the amendment's substance into a series of absolute statements concerning its benefits and flaws. Consider the plight of the state legislator holding in her/his hand a copy of two fliers—one coming from Stop ERA, the other from the National Association of Women Lawyers, and *both* entitled "What the Equal Rights Amendment Means." Selected sections:

Stop ERA	National Association of Women Lawyers
1. ERA will make every wife in the U.S. legally responsible to provide 50% of the financial support of her family.	1. ERA will require State domestic relations laws to treat women as equals; thus State laws will necessarily require *either* spouse to provide a home or financial support for the homemaker of his or her family.
2. ERA will wipe out a woman's present freedom of choice to take a paying job *or* to be a fulltime wife and mother supported by her husband.	2. ERA will not deprive any woman of the right to be a mother and/or homemaker but will enhance the status of her position giving her equal partnership in the marriage.
3. ERA could create havoc in prisons and reform schools by preventing segregation of the sexes.	3. ERA will not affect the constitutional right of privacy recognizing the need for segrega-
4. ERA does not guarantee women better paying jobs, promotions, or better working	

conditions. The Equal Employment Opportunity Act and other laws already guarantee women "equal pay for equal work" and need only to be enforced to ensure women equal opportunity.

tion of the sexes in public and school restrooms.

4. ERA will guarantee to men as well as women equal rights to equal pay for equal work and the right to equal opportunity.

Struggling under this barrage of contradictory information, one Montana state legislator shifted the whole decision to God by reasoning that if He had wanted women to be equal, He would have had six female apostles. Or take the case of the woman legislator from a western state who refused to give any deeper rationale for her "no" vote beyond "I like having men open doors for me." And despite the often intemperate tone of the opposition groups' attacks on the ERA, such have had a strong impact on many legislators, as is reflected in the following exchanges during floor debate and subsequent personal statements:

> There will be no more girls' schools. The House of the Good Shepherd for wayward girls, I suppose, can be inhabited by anybody looking for a room for the night. Ah ... convents, I don't know what will become of them, but they'll be unconstitutional, I suppose. States which grant jury service exemptions to women with children will either extend the exemption to men with children or abolish the exemption altogether. So, try and get a jury sometime. They'll be composed of bachelors, I suppose, and not if they tell the truth. (An Illinois opponent)

> I have seen the courts of the United States usurp the Legislative power to the point where I can envision an army with a hundred men being ordered to take their guns and go down to the trenches and to go forward and they retreat because there is not a single woman among them. And they rush into court and get an order and say our constitutional rights are being violated because no women are digging ditches, no women are down here fighting, they're all punching typewriters and we're doing all the fighting and therefore, it's unequal and unconstitutional. (An Illinois opponent)

> The ERA will take all the beauty, all the good things out of womanhood and will lower women to a lower plane than men. It would absolutely abolish segregated washrooms, would abso-

lutely draft them, subject them to manual labor. It will end support, alimony, and child support. We can comply all we need in Georgia; we don't need to tie this to the national group. If ratified, it will get women in this one central agency, under one central control, and that's all the Communist Party will need to control America. (A Georgia opponent)

To supporters, the ERA was to be an important but benign implement for removing the legal barriers to female equality. Many opponents, however, firmly believed that those three initials stood for "Evil Rules America." With the existence of two diametrically opposed interpretations of the amendment, the potential for major conflict in the states was distinct.

On June 21, 1972, when nationwide ratification still seemed certain, members of the Massachusetts lower house could lightheartedly play a joke on supporters in the galleries by turning on their red ("NO") lights before switching to ratify the amendment, 205–7. Massachusetts was the 20th state to ratify and the time for such games was almost over. Partisans on both sides quickly became deadly serious as both sides settled in for a protracted struggle. By the end of the legislative sessions of 1978, several threats or acts of violence had occurred. In Michigan, after a house committee rejected a rescission resolution, amendment opponents stormed the podium, warning committee members: "We'll get rid of the gun control proposal and then we'll blow every one of your heads off." In Louisiana a group calling itself the Southern Belles broke windows and spray-painted the word "PIG" on the New Orleans homes of two legislative opponents, dramatically leaving behind threatening letters fashioned from old newspaper clippings.[3] In Virginia two ERA supporters were arrested for disorderly conduct, trespassing, and assaulting a police officer after the amendment was defeated in a house committee. Proponents of the amendment, who by and large had used traditional lobbying techniques to obtain congressional passage, did not always confine themselves to such tactics in the drive for ratification. During the legislative recess in the summer of 1972, James Mills, state senator of California, who had earlier effectively stalled the ERA in his Senate Rules Committee, found members of women's groups raising the issue of the ERA at all of his public appearances.

The National Organization for Women (NOW) held demonstrations on the steps of his office. And as he prepared to undertake a statewide bicycle tour as a prelude to a possible 1974 gubernatorial bid, members of NOW announced that they, too, would get on their bicycles and accompany him. On November 8, 1972, the ERA passed out of Mills' committee and was quickly ratified. Although fighting a rearguard action in this instance, opposition groups signaled that they, too, would not be bound by conventional strategies. On November 10, 1972, five members of the California-based Happiness of Womanhood arrived at the capitol in Sacramento to present to each of the 29 senators who had voted for the amendment gaily beribboned boxes containing live white mice and notes reading, "Do you want to be a man or a mouse?"

Direct action for and against the ERA became commonplace in the states thereafter. Parades, rallies, pickets, and sit-ins—all were used as overt demonstrations of personal convictions on the issue. Women in Cincinnati staged a "ride for rights" on roller skates and bicycles in the downtown area in 1973. That same year, Florida senators were startled to find their chamber doorway blocked by six rain-drenched NOW members in floor-length mourning clothes, carrying a casket in protest against the lack of senate action on the amendment. In 1974, even "street theater" came to the floor of the Tennessee house, with the permission of the speaker, as members watched opposition group members present a devastatingly bitter ten-minute skit panning the ERA.

Political Conflict

In this study of the conditions surrounding the ratification of the proposed Equal Rights Amendment, two complementary models of political conflict are used. One is descriptive of traditional interest group politics; the other is associated with a more rancorous form of political conflict, that of "community conflict." Conflict, one of the key concepts in political science, is central to a principal function of government itself: conflict management on matters of public importance. Government decision makers authoritatively resolve issues which are contested within the polity.

It has been observed that politics in America is particularly vulnerable to conflict because of its openness, dispersion of power, and the social cleavages on which it rests. These characteristics in turn encourage citizens to advance claims, lodge objections, and wield influence. But despite this potentially dynamic relationship between competing parties, the policy process in America is generally conceded to have a strong conservative bias. Policies change slowly, if at all, and then only incrementally. Only a small percentage of all potential issues is ever publicly debated. Some are screened out by an existing consensus in society. Others are prevented from receiving public exposure through the use of conflict management techniques. Conflict and controversy thus periodically serve to force items onto the agenda and, in doing so, prevent stagnation, readjust the balance of power, and form the basis for personal and social change.

In the case of the ERA—an issue which had received no hearing in Congress since 1956—Senator Birch Bayh (D.-Ind.) admitted that the 1970 Senate hearings on the matter were the direct result of an earlier confrontation between his Subcommittee on Constitutional Amendments and a group of ERA advocates. On February 17, 1970, during hearings on what was to become the Twenty-sixth Amendment (to enfranchise eighteen-year-olds), Wilma Scott Heide, chair-one[4] of the board of directors of NOW, and about twenty other women had disrupted the proceedings and demanded that hearings be scheduled on the Equal Rights Amendment.[5]

But governmental decision makers do not merely react to the demands of extragovernmental groups or sit as referees or judges as such groups compete, detached from the conflict. Frequently legislators and other decision makers are themselves participants in group conflicts. That this was true of the conflict over the ERA is evident in the statements of legislators such as those quoted above.

At this point, it should be noted that "conflict" and "competition" are generally to be used interchangeably. Mack and Snyder, however, have suggested a conceptual distinction which is useful in differentiating the two models of political conflict used here.[6] "Competition," narrowly defined, takes place only in accordance with existing sets of rules governing the tactics to be used by those seeking to obtain scarce resources. "Conflict" occurs when competitors disregard these rules or when they seek to destroy each other in their quest for scarce resources. Since much of the behavior of ERA activists falls in between and is neither clearly competition nor purely conflict, no sharp dichotomy between the two terms will be formulated.

The interest group conflict model used here assumes that only those groups adopting institutionally approved and provided means (i.e., engaging in "competition") will be successful. This conforms to the "insider strategy" of pluralist politics. Increasingly, this pluralist conception of agenda building and decision making has been challenged by those who suggest that when competitors use unorthodox methods (i.e., engage in "conflict"), they may have a greater chance of forcing decision makers to consider their position.[7] The "outsider strategy" involving violation of the established techniques of pluralist politics, it is argued, is not self-defeating per se. Some political disputes are resolved in a broader public arena (the "community"), beyond the complete control of interest groups. This second type of group conflict/competition is most commonly called "community conflict."

The attempt at ratification of the ERA can be viewed as a process involving interaction between state legislators and interested publics. To the extent that these interactions were confined to those between legislators and members of organized groups participating in the political process through the established channels of the lobbying system, the conflict is that of traditional interest group politics. And a number of such organizations were involved in the ERA campaign. However, the appearance of numerous ad hoc groups following congressional passage of the ERA suggests that members of the community who ordinarily are not engaged in making demands upon decision makers through established channels had been drawn into this particular conflict. When the scope of conflict expands into the larger political community in this fashion, the dynamics of community conflict become controlling.

Two distinct types of groups—each associated with a different model of conflict—appear to have been active in the state ERA ratification campaigns. Furthermore, each model has different implications concerning the nature, dynamics, and resolution of conflict in the public arena.

The Interest Group Conflict Model

The study of interest groups has a long and controversial history in political science.[8] Both scholars and journalists have attributed to "pressure groups" and "the lobby" great influence in the legislative process. More recently, studies of interest group activity have expressed doubts about the abilities and effectiveness of such organizations. One criticism is that groups are poorly financed and their lobbying campaigns are ill-timed, coming after most decision makers have reached a definitive position.[9] More accurately, groups are neither omnipotent nor totally without influence in the legislative process. In some areas, such as civil liberties and civil rights policies, constituency groups appear to be an integral part of the decision process; in other areas, such as government management, legislators appear to operate relatively free of group influence.[10] Since the ERA is basically a civil rights issue, it was anticipated that groups would play an influential role in the decision on ERA ratification in the states.

Lobbying may be defined as any effort on the part of any individual or group to influence political elites by direct persuasion (e.g., letter writing or personal interactions) or indirect persuasion (e.g., organizing at the constituency level or through the mass media).[11] Lobbyists might utilize a variety of activities and techniques: personal lobbying, presentation of research, hearings testimony, contacts by constituents and legislative "friends," letter and telegram campaigns, public relations campaigns, publicizing voting records, entertaining, bribery, and election-oriented tactics such as contributing time or money to a legislator's campaign.

According to the model, one tactic potentially available to interest groups—that of electoral threats—historically has rarely been used. Although Presthus found that governmental elites clearly perceive some groups as potentially sanction-ing,[12] observers of interest groups generally feel that most organizations try to convey the impression of political power without actually going to the trouble and expense of attempt-ing to defeat someone at the polls. Legislators' resistance may only be intensified by electoral threats. Furthermore, the abil-ity of mass membership organizations to deliver their mem-bers' votes on election day is quite limited. Schattschneider has estimated that, at a maximum, only 20 percent of any group's vote can be attributed to that group's efforts at mobilization.[13] For a small-membership group, as were al-most all the groups active in the ERA ratification campaign, this translates into relatively few votes. An additional hand-icap for interest groups wishing to participate in electoral politics is the fact that most such groups cannot freely change their allegiance from one major party to the other. Each of the major parties attracts a loose constellation of interest groups and these alignments tend to be very stable. But despite these barriers, many groups active in ERA ratification, particularly proponent groups, chose to use electoral sanctions against legislators in disagreement with them. Regardless of their relatively small memberships, further, women's groups may have been advantaged in that due to their relatively recent entry into partisan politics, none are firmly established as either major party's "constellations."[14]

Students of interest groups have often noted that intensive lobbying is directed at only a few individuals—the unde-cided, members of committees, and other pivotal people in the legislative process such as legislative leaders. Concentra-tion on the committees considering a measure is generally a good strategy for reasons beyond mere conservation of time and energy. Committees shape legislation, and traditionally members of committees are likely to be basically sympathetic to associated group interests (e.g., pro-agriculture legislators usually serve on the Agriculture Committee; pro-education legislators are commonly found on the Education Commit-tee). In the case of the ERA, however, no such symbiotic rela-tionship existed between legislators and interest groups on either side of the issue. Still, it was to be expected that both proponent and opponent groups would expend considerable energy in working for a committee report on the ERA consistent with their views.

A basic characteristic of all groups participating in interest group politics is a strong upper middle-class bias.[15] Most such groups are disproportionately composed of persons of higher status rather than a cross section of those whose interest or occupation is ostensibly represented. Schattschneider has estimated that 90 percent of the population cannot get into the pressure system.[16] Furthermore, this system is limited to those "legitimate" groups which have already gained access to the political arena. Within this context of an elitist bias, however, certain factors are felt to be related to each interest group's effectiveness. Longley has suggested five of these: the interest group's potentialities, its goals, its maximization of resources, its tactics, and its relations with other groups.[17]

An interest group's potentialities are determined largely by the group's place in society and such internal characteristics as formal organization and cohesiveness. Groups drawing their membership from higher social strata are presumed to be more "legitimate" and thus more effective. Legitimacy is also a function of membership size, a rough indication of the extent to which that group can realistically claim as members the population it seeks to represent. The geographical area from which a group draws its membership is crucial as well. Unless an interest group has some direct connection with the legislators' constituencies, it will have little or no influence upon their decisions. The age of an organization is also important. An older group presumably has built up popular support, developed political liaisons, and achieved an established place in the community. Finally, such organizational characteristics as a formal bureaucratic structure, a permanent staff with technical and political skills, a well-developed communications system, and a cohesive and mobilized membership are considered assets in influencing legislators. Presthus found, however, that of the above size and effectiveness of organization were the critical ingredients of group success. Legitimacy, on the other hand, was not always associated with influence. Legislators do not necessarily have to perceive lobbyists as being legitimate in order to be subject to their influence.[18] This would suggest that the ad hoc groups formed in opposition to the ERA might be able to overcome the hypothetical advantages of the more reputable, longer-established proponent groups through superior organization and mobilization of membership.

Another factor in interest group success is goals that are generally congruent with the prevailing value system in society or, at the least, are compatible with the values held by the decision makers. Aside from this possible constraint, however, a group's purpose or orientation (change versus status quo) is not necessarily crucial to a group's success.[19] Still, one advantage may accrue to the change-oriented groups in that, as one study indicates, such groups tend to be more active than are those groups seeking to maintain the status quo.[20]

Level of interest group activity is one indicator of the maximization of group resources. Presthus found that groups with highly active lobbyists were most effective. In fact, he concluded that this was probably the most important characteristic of the influential interest group.[21] A group's ability to obtain adequate amounts of money to support its activities is also considered essential for group success. A third group resource of interest here is leverage to provide or withhold resources that government needs. This may be expert knowledge or even the ability to block policy implementation by refusal to cooperate. The more potentially disruptive the group, the greater is its bargaining power.

Few groups have the genuine power to prevent policy implementation, however, and disruptive tactics alone are often viewed as illegitimate by decision makers. Groups using such dramatic tactics as protest rallies not only breach the political "rules of the game" but also risk alienating decision makers who themselves are accustomed to very different interpersonal styles. Instead, the most successful group tactics appear to be those involving services to legislators, particularly the presentation of information and research.[22]

A final factor in the success of an interest group is the extent to which it forms ties and alliances with other groups and key individuals of compatible interests. Nearly all governmental decision makers will be hesitant to disregard the demands of a strong coalition of groups.[23] Cooperation among groups is believed to increase the power, access, and tactical advantages of the groups while decreasing the financial and political risks for any of the individual groups. But elite support is important; decision makers value other elites' opinions even more than they value public and group opinion.

Because much interest group activity occurs in the absence of any competition from opposing interest groups, interest group effectiveness is most frequently determined by the factors described above, rather than by the relative strengths and abilities of competing groups. Kingdon, in his study of congressional lobbying, found that competition between groups on a given issue was reported only 12 percent of the time.[24] Although groups faced with an organized opposition tend themselves to become more active, more highly organized, and more cohesive,[25] the presence of group conflict acts as a constraint upon policy adoption.

When no controversy surrounds an issue and group pressure is exerted in only one direction, the model suggests that the decision maker will most often vote *with* the group to adopt or reject the new policy. Where group conflict does arise, the decision process will be slowed as the legislators must weigh the relative political strengths of both sides. In the case of the ERA it was expected that in the absence of opposition, those interest groups active on behalf of the ERA were usually successful provided that they conformed to the profile of the effective interest group. In those states where organized opposition to the ERA appeared, predictions of legislative decision making were based on a comparison of the two opposing groups or coalitions, taking into consideration the extent to which each side approximated the model of the effective interest group.

The Community Conflict Model

The community conflict model allows predictions about the formation of public policy based on certain characteristics assumed to be common to all such conflicts. The model provides descriptions of participants in a conflict, the dynamics of a conflict once begun, and the issues most likely to embroil a community in conflict. Finally, the model suggests the impact such conflicts have upon decision makers and upon the policy process.[26] Most research dealing with community conflict has focused upon conflicts occurring in cities or rural communities. Therefore, inferences drawn from this model are not always applicable to a statewide controversy such as the ERA.

The community conflict model shares a number of assumptions with the interest group conflict model in respect to the factors of group effectiveness. The community conflict model, however, does not contain the latter model's elitist bias. Those who participate in community conflicts are not necessarily members of the organized groups having regular access to the pressure group system. At its height, a community conflict will have drawn an unusually high percentage of the entire community into active participation, and, at a minimum, most community members will be at least aware of the conflict and its possible consequences.

Students of two of the most recurrent subjects of community conflicts in the past twenty years—the fluoridation of water and civil rights—have found that organizations and individuals from outside the community have played substantial roles in the initiation and expansion of conflict. Particularly in the case of fluoridation—an issue sharing many remarkable parallels with the conflict over ERA ratification—the national opposition forces were formally organized and connected by a preexisting communication network formed for other political purposes but easily channeled into the antifluoridation effort. Local opposition campaigns were buttressed by nationally prepared literature and personal appearances by national opposition leaders, much as the ultra-conservative American Right, led by Phyllis Schlafly, has mobilized local residents against the ERA in numerous communities in the states.

Another observation concerning the personal characteristics of leaders of community conflicts—one which directly contradicts the assumptions of the interest group conflict model—is that those persons with the *lowest* social status often appear to be most effective, particularly when they are seeking to block the adoption of a policy. In the case of fluoridation, proponents were consistently better-educated, better-known in the community, of higher occupational status, and more politically experienced than were the opponents, yet fluoridation had a failure rate of about 60 percent, 1950–60. Furthermore, opponents who were the least educated and least known proved to be most efficacious, perhaps because they were less constrained by the political rules of the game and less hesitant to use the most dramatic, even irrational, arguments (e.g., fluoridation causes nymphomania).

Participants in community conflicts appear to illustrate Gresham's Law of Conflict. To wit, the harmful and dangerous elements drive out those (i.e., community leaders and established organizations) who would keep the conflict in bounds. Elite support of group goals is assumed to be essential to group effectiveness, as in the interest group conflict model. But in a community conflict established community leaders and organizations often withdraw from the conflict or become neutralized. Elite support is particularly essential to those seeking adoption of a new policy, since it serves to legitimate the policy. Neutrality, or even the lack of *active* support, may cause the public to conclude that something is wrong with the proposal. Similarly, when those with technical or professional expertise on the issue in dispute (in the case of the ERA, constitutional scholars) refuse to participate in the debate, the impact on the public may be the same.

Although established community organizations may be drawn into the conflict, such groups often remain neutral in order to avoid internal conflicts. If a position of neutrality is adopted, there arises the need for new partisan organizations, formed on an ad hoc basis, to contest the issue. These organizations and their leaders, lacking any previous position in the community, are less likely to contain the conflict.

Other participants in the community conflict are the mass media. As Coleman has observed, many controversies are born when community members unsuspectingly open their newspapers one morning.[27] The local media are not only significant in the initial stages of a controversy, but also continue to be influential by conveying each side's views and actions to the community as a whole. Once an issue has captured the interest of the media, greater and greater attention is generally accorded it. Although editorial support is welcomed by partisans on both sides, the media are relatively unimportant in influencing the direction of public opinion in comparison, for example, with conversations between friends. The local media instead often serve to legitimate both sides, no matter how deviant or extremist, by granting them both publicity.

The community conflict model suggests that, as the controversy expands, the original issues which touched off the conflict will undergo major transformations, primarily due to the efforts of the weaker side. Complex issues are simplified and distorted in order to appeal to the general public.[28] New and different issues, unrelated to the original ones, are introduced in order to attract new participants by substituting one controversy for another.[29] This is most likely to occur when one side is at a great disadvantage by the definition of the issues (e.g., when the ERA is equated solely with the positive symbol "equality") but has potential strength if the debate can be extended to other topics (e.g., the politically conservative issues of states' rights and anticommunism). Finally, with the widening of conflict, the tone of the debate shifts to one of antagonism, personal slander, and overt hostility.

In the case of such an expanded controversy, the community conflict model further suggests that the side working for the adoption of a new policy is at a great disadvantage. Proponent campaigns almost inevitably are defensive in nature even though change-oriented partisans recognize that counterpropaganda is tactically inferior to a strong positive appeal. Even objective educational campaigns allowing the "true facts" to speak for themselves are likely, in the context of a heated community conflict, to be self-defeating. What is actually said is less crucial than the fact that an argument is going on. The burden of proof rests with those seeking change; those who seek to block adoption of that policy need only create a reasonable doubt in the public mind. Even when an opposition charge is discredited, opponents can quickly advance a new argument in its place. Public education campaigns often confuse the general public and can even reverse preexisting favorable opinions toward the policy.

Those seeking adoption of a public policy which has become the center of public controversy thus face a dilemma. If proponents mount a direct attack upon the opposition, they risk lending the opposition arguments greater prominence than they otherwise might receive and, in the process, raise the level of controversy. On the other hand, if proponents avoid public debate, they are vulnerable to charges of using elitist and undemocratic tactics and of suppressing the other side of the issue.

The model also suggests that a further disadvantage faced by proponents is that the controversial policy they support is, at root, only a surrogate issue for those most active in the opposition. Opponents perceive the proposed policy to be in conflict with their basic views concerning government, society, and change itself (i.e., with their ideology). Community conflicts are, then, ideological struggles, with all the inherent bitterness and intransigence of such clashes.

Given this linkage between ideology and community conflict, certain types of issues, according to the community conflict model, can easily be converted into full-scale conflicts. Cobb and Elder have suggested a number of features facilitating the development of conflict.[30] Issues which can be defined broadly to appeal to more subgroups within the population are more likely to become the subject of conflict. Subjects presented in abstract terms such as "equality," "equal protection of the laws," "justice," and "civil rights"—as has been true of the ERA—are easily expanded to a broader audience. Issues perceived as being of general and enduring social significance are also more likely to be surrounded by conflict than are those which are of short-range relevance to a more limited public. In general, the more nontechnical the definition of a topic, the greater the likelihood that it will reach a larger public. In the case of a controversial issue initially argued on technical or complex legal grounds, contradictory information supplied by both sides' "experts" ultimately forces a nontechnical definition of the issue. Finally, issues appearing to lack a clear precedent are more likely than others to become the subject of community conflict.

The scope of conflict is important in that it is assumed to have a strong impact upon decision makers. As in the interest group conflict model, the presence of conflict itself makes it more difficult for decision makers to create policies which would resolve the conflict. In fact, the higher the level of controversy, the greater the likelihood that decision makers will take no action on the policy. This institutional tendency toward inertia again most affects those who seek adoption of the policy.

Decision makers, however, cannot prevent a community conflict from appearing on the political agenda. The possibility for nondecision making is removed; decision makers must consider and reconsider the issue until it is resolved.[31] Decision making on the ERA is made even more difficult since it is not a compromisable issue in the way that pieces of legislation often are; it must either be accepted or rejected in its entirety.

As described by the community conflict model, decision makers, forced to respond publicly in some manner, frequently choose to sidestep the basic issue, at least temporarily. They may act on one aspect of the issue (e.g., passage of antidiscrimination legislation), create new organizational units to deal with the problem (e.g., a state commission on the status of women), or postpone action until additional information is received (e.g., create a special legislative study committee). The model would indicate that such actions are rational alternatives given the ambiguity and misgivings surrounding controversial issues and the uncertain political consequences accompanying definitive policy making. Decision makers may be just as confused as the general public on matters of community conflict. In the case of the ERA, a legislator, perplexed about its ultimate impact, might reasonably have felt there would be less danger for society in a "no" vote since ratification could occur later. It is also possible that the seven-year period instituted for ratification encouraged a "go-slow" mentality among decision makers.

Politically, decision makers have no real way to assess either side's strength since rarely are the leaders in community conflicts those persons with whom decision makers ordinarily interact. The community conflict model suggests that in the absence of such information decision makers will be wary of offending *anyone*; the issue simply is not worth even the smallest political risk. The losing side conceivably could become a major opposition force in the next election.

In summary, the community conflict model seems to provide insights into several of the most puzzling aspects of the history of ERA ratification. It not only explains the appearance of the ad hoc opposition groups, such as Stop ERA and Happiness of Womanhood, but also indicates several reasons for their remarkable success with the general public and decision makers in many states, despite the apparent intemperance and irrelevance of many of their charges against the ERA.

Methodology

The case-study method was used to assess the applicability of these two conflict models to the politics of ERA ratification. Field research was done during a four-month period, January–May 1974, in three states: Texas, Georgia, and Illinois. Only states whose legislatures were in session in 1974 were considered as research sites. These states were selected because their dissimilar decisions on the ERA reflected the range of legislative responses to that issue.

The *Urban Affairs Library*, consisting of clippings from one or more newspapers published in each of the 50 states was used to classify responses to the ERA. (See table 1.2.) Criteria used were: direction (ratification or nonratification) and speed of legislative action; legislative consensus as reflected in roll-call votes; and the level of intergroup conflict reported by the media. In the original research design, Connecticut, a state that ratified after initially rejecting the amendment, was also chosen as a site for fieldwork. Later it was decided that there were insufficient conceptual differences in intergroup conflict and legislative consensus between late-ratifying states, such as Connecticut, and unratified states, such as Illinois, to justify this additional commitment of resources. At that time, and as of this writing, there was also a strong possibility that Illinois, too, would ratify the amendment.

Texas was a state where quick and decisive ratification did occur. It was the eighth state to ratify the ERA, doing so during a special session, March 28–30, 1972, by a margin of 133–9 in the house and by unanimous voice vote in the senate. Legislators reported little or no lobbying by interest groups;

Table 1.2
Typology of State Responses to the ERA, 1972–78

I	II	III	IV
Quick ratifica-tion[1] High/moderate consensus Moderate/low conflict	Delayed ratifi-cation[2] No pattern of consensus High conflict	Nonratification Low consensus High conflict	Nonratification High/moderate consensus High/moderate conflict
Alaska	Connecticut	Florida	Alabama
California	Indiana	Illinois	Arizona
Colorado	Maine	Missouri	Arkansas
Delaware	Montana	Nevada	Georgia
Hawaii	North Dakota	North Carolina	Louisiana
Idaho	Ohio	South Carolina	Mississippi
Iowa	Vermont	Virginia	Oklahoma
Kansas			Utah
Kentucky			
Maryland			
Massachusetts			
Michigan			
Minnesota			
Nebraska			
New Hampshire			
New Jersey			
New Mexico			
New York			
Oregon			
Pennsylvania			
Rhode Island			
South Dakota			
Tennessee			
Texas			
Washington			
West Virginia			
Wisconsin			
Wyoming			

[1]Ratified in 1972 or 1973 on first vote.
[2]Ratified after one or more votes to reject.

most group leaders reported they were caught by surprise during this short session. It should not be assumed, however, that the Texas legislature was filled with women's rights advocates. Note the response of one legislator who voted against it:

> Thirty to forty legislators told me privately they were against that damn thing but they'd better not vote against it right before the primary. There weren't nine votes against it, there were about ninety but that's how many didn't have the guts to vote against it. One told me, "It's dumb, it's stupid, it's not going to help the women but . . . to hell with them."

Even so, there was no serious move against the amendment in Texas until 1975, when a resolution to rescind died in committee.

In *Georgia*, as in many of the Deep South states, the ERA has encountered significantly greater opposition than support in the legislature. The Georgia house voted for the first time on the ERA in 1974, decisively defeating it, 70–104. It reached the senate floor in 1975 and was rejected there as well. The amendment had been placed in a special study committee in the house in 1973, disappointing proponent group members who had put much effort in 1972 into obtaining written pledges from state legislative candidates to support the ERA in the next session. Because more than 100 legislators-elect, a comfortable majority, had signed these forms, up to the end of January 1973, these groups expected a routine ratification, but, as one proponent explained:

> Over *one* weekend, the legislators on Monday came back and said, "No way, no way." The letters had come in here. Thousands and thousands of dollars [were spent in Georgia]. I can't prove it, but the figure $40,000 was thrown out by Mrs. Schlafly herself at one time.

The group alignment on the ERA in Georgia covers a surprisingly broad range. In opposition are members of Stop ERA, the American Party, and the John Birch Society, doing their best to disassociate themselves from J. B. Stoner, chairperson of the National States' Rights Party and a voluble opponent of the amendment. In support are such traditional groups as the League of Women Voters and the American Association of University Women, as well as the Atlanta Lesbian Feminist Alliance and the Socialist Workers Party.

Illinois is typical of those states whose legislature is or has been closely divided over the amendment. In some, the ERA has now been ratified after initial rejection. In others, like Illinois, ratification has not yet occurred, despite strong support in the legislature. In Illinois, the legislature has voted several times on the ERA. Yet only twice have supporters been able to muster the required majority. With the legislature so deeply divided on the issue and the understandable frustrations stemming from this long effort, the Illinois campaign has also been one of the most bitter. The personal attacks begun by Representative Tom Hanahan in May 1972, when he characterized ERA supporters as "braless, brainless broads," were answered with the printing of bumper stickers labeling certain legislators "male chauvinist pigs."

In each of the three states, I interviewed the leaders or spokespersons of those groups most active in supporting or in opposing the ERA, as well as those members of the legislature who were generally recognized as the amendment's main proponents and opponents. Also queried were other "influentials" in the ratification process, such as legislative committee chairpersons, legislative leaders, governors, and the chairpersons of the state commissions on the status of women. In all, 78 interviews were conducted. (Appendix A shows the distribution of the respondents by sex, role, and state residence.) They consisted of a loosely structured set of open-ended questions and ranged in length from 15 minutes to an hour and one-half. Most ran from 30 to 40 minutes. (See Appendixes B and C for the interview guides.)

Most interviews in Georgia and Texas took place in Atlanta and Austin, respectively, although a limited number of phone interviews with Texans outside Austin was conducted. Only in Illinois was it necessary to conduct fieldwork in two cities, Springfield, the state capital, and Chicago, where many of the group leaders lived. No prospective respondent refused to be interviewed. With only three exceptions, interviewees consented to the use of a tape recorder. This allowed not only greater accuracy but also closer scheduling between interviews. Even so, I found that it was not possible, given the problems of transportation in a metropolitan area, to meet with every interviewee. Thus, a limited number of phone interviews were conducted.

Through these interviews I hoped to determine the relative predictive/explanatory strengths of the two conflict models as applied to the politics of ERA ratification. The focus of the interviews was upon the key elements of each conflict model: the personal characteristics of those group members who had become involved with the ERA and their past political experience; the role of established organizations and that of new groups, if any, that formed around this issue; the patterns of cooperation which developed between like-minded groups; group strategies, tactics, and resources; and the extent of support for both sides among the general public and elites outside the legislature. Also of interest was the dynamics of the controversy over the ERA and what effect that had had on legislative reactions. What was the role of the media? What issues (related and unrelated) were raised by each side? Did the ERA gain or lose support in the legislature with changes in the level of intergroup conflict? Finally, what was the legislature's official response to the ERA?

Given the varied responses to the ERA in the 50 states, it was predicted that in general the interest group conflict model was more descriptive of the amendment's supporters and their activities, particularly in the early-ratifying states, and that the community conflict model was more adaptable for explaining the activities and impact of the ERA's opponents.

For example, where ratification encountered difficulty, a core of politically experienced women's groups, including the League of Women Voters and the Business and Professional Women's Clubs, was active in its behalf. The national headquarters of these groups had set aside special ERA funds. They were skilled in the use of the media; their literature and press releases were professional in appearance and rational in tone. In almost every state there was a large umbrella coalition, some containing over 100 member organizations, working for the ERA. Frequently, full-time lobbyists were employed in the state capitals. Endorsement of the ERA from numerous state and local elected officials, including almost every state's governor, had been obtained. In short, these were groups having many of the characteristics of the "winners" described by the interest group conflict model. And, it should be remembered, the ERA *had* been ratified in 35 of 50 states by 1977.

On the other hand, many states have failed to ratify and others did so only after long and bitter debate. And in these states the politics of the ERA is apparently well-described by the community conflict model. Many ad hoc local and state groups sprang up in opposition to the amendment. Whether accurately or not, the leaders of such ad hoc groups have portrayed themselves as politically inexperienced "housewives and mothers." They have been very successful in controlling the tone and content of the debate by forcing proponent groups onto the defensive. ERA supporters have been forced to reply to questions concerning coed restrooms and homosexual marriages, as well as to defend their own group's stance on logically unrelated issues such as abortion and prostitution. Merely by responding to such inquiries seriously, proponents have enhanced the doubts and controversy surrounding the amendment. Even though proponents have been able to obtain formal statements of support from many prominent community and state leaders, the presence of an opposition movement seems to have sometimes discouraged these leaders from actively seeking support for the amendment within the legislature.

A second purpose of the case studies was to evaluate the role of women and women's groups as participants in the political process. The ERA ratification campaign has been unusual in that most of the actively lobbying groups (on both sides) have been composed primarily of women. This phenomenon may have implications for both conflict models—in particular the emphasis each places on "political amateurs" and "group legitimacy," primarily of women. Thus it is not surprising that sex roles and even innuendoes concerning acts of sex seem to have exercised a distinct influence upon the politics of the ERA.

Take the case, for example, of the Florida state male legis-

lator who became enraged at having received an obscene ges-
ture from a female supporter of the amendment. Undoubtedly
the sex of the offending party was a factor in the incident
having become a public issue. Or consider the charge by some
Georgia male legislators, opposed to the ERA, that women
representing proponent groups were exposing their legs and
propositioning the legislators on the floor of the house!

This is not to suggest that women did not use sex, or, rather,
traditional femininity, as a weapon to influence the legislators. In the past few years, Illinois legislators have received
homemade bread, cookies, and small apple pies from Stop
ERA members. In 1974, in the box along with the apple pie
was a card picturing a "feminine" woman on the front and
containing a poem inside: "I enjoy being a girl / My heart and
my hand / went into this dough / For the sake of the family /
please vote 'no.'"

In response, many proponents have adopted the strategy of
"out-ladying" the opposition by also proffering food, flowers,
and cards. They have been particularly careful to wear
dresses or skirts when approaching legislators. Some groups
reportedly have even chosen their most physically attractive
members to lobby the most resistant opponents.

Whether or not these appeals to the masculine libido have
been successful is debatable. The fact remains that much hostility still exists toward women in this society. Inevitably this
has been reflected in the ERA ratification campaigns. For
example, all legislators historically have experienced heavy
and persistent lobbying on issues of high intergroup conflict
and public controversy. One wonders, however, if the Ohio
legislature's response to such lobbying on the ERA has a precedent. On the day of the house committee hearing and vote
on the ERA, the Ohio legislature ordered the women's restrooms in the state capitol in Columbus locked and had
"out-of-order" signs placed on the elevators. Then there was
the incident in Minnesota, involving a sit-in in the men's
room of the state capitol in St. Paul by a group of high school
girls to protest the possibility of integrated restrooms with
the ERA. The sergeant-at-arms, worrying about how to remove the young women, was advised by one legislator, "Pee
on them."

Throughout this discussion of the politics of the ERA in the states, sex is considered a possible intervening variable in the decision-making process. It is possible that the legislators' perceptions of and responses to lobbying were influenced by the lobbyists' gender and that in turn may have affected their choice of tactics. It is also conceivable that the ERA was seen as a "women's issue" and thus was singled out by the legislators for treatment different from that which any controversial issue would receive.

Plan of the Book

Chapter 2 discusses the Equal Rights Amendment in terms of its legislative history, its varying legal interpretations, and the development of broad-based public support for its principles. The remaining chapters examine the controversy in which the ERA became embroiled: chapter 3 scrutinizes the participants in the controversy and the organizational structures within which they operated; chapter 4 explores the tactics of the lobbying campaigns mounted by ERA's supporters and opponents; chapter 5 describes the decision process primarily from the perspective of interest group members and state legislators. The Epilogue presents conclusions concerning the ERA and the nature of governmental decision making on issues of public controversy.

NOTES

1. *The John Birch Society Bulletin*, May 1973, p. 25.
2. Quoted in "ERA—Selling Womanhood Short," *Christian Crusade Weekly* 14 (10 March 1974): 3.
3. Another Louisiana legislator claimed that this group threatened to assassinate her and bomb her house unless she became a supporter of the amendment. However, an ERA supporter in Louisiana discounted this. The Southern Belles apparently are radical feminists who do support the ERA but also wish to discredit other proponent groups, particularly the National Organization for Women.
4. This is the designation used by the National Organization for Women.
5. Reported in Judith Hole and Ellen Levine, *Rebirth of Feminism* (New York: Quadrangle, 1971), pp. 55–56.

6. Raymond W. Mack and Richard C. Snyder, "The Analysis of Social Conflict: Toward an Overview and Synthesis," *Journal of Conflict Resolution* 1 (June 1957): 217.
7. See Roger W. Cobb and Charles D. Elder, *Participation in American Politics: The Dynamics of Agenda–Building* (Boston: Allyn & Bacon, 1972) and William A. Gamson, *The Strategy of Social Protest* (Homewood, Ill.: Dorsey, 1975).
8. Two major studies are: Arthur A. Bentley, *The Process of Government* (Bloomington, Ind.: Principia, 1949) and David Truman, *The Governmental Process* (New York: Knopf, 1951).
9. See Raymond A. Bauer et al., *American Business and Public Policy* (New York: Atherton, 1963); and Lester Milbrath, *The Washington Lobbyists* (Chicago: Rand McNally, 1963).
10. See Aage R. Clausen, *How Congressmen Decide: A Policy Focus* (New York: St. Martin's, 1973).
11. Robert Presthus, *Elites in the Policy Process* (New York: Cambridge University Press, 1974), p. 213.
12. Ibid., p. 216.
13. E. E. Schattschneider, *The Semi-Sovereign People* (New York: Holt, Rinehart and Winston, 1960), p. 52.
14. This is particularly true of the determinedly nonpartisan League of Women Voters and the more conservative Business and Professional Women's Clubs. However, a 1974 survey of the membership of the National Organization for Women showed that 53 percent described themselves as Democrats, while only 15 percent were self-labeled Republicans. The National Women's Political Caucus, too, has suffered from being perceived as a part of the liberal wing of the Democratic Party. See Jeane J. Kirkpatrick, *Political Woman* (New York: Basic, 1974), pp. 164–65.
15. See Charles R. Wright and Herbert H. Hyman, "Voluntary Association Memberships of American Adults: Evidence from National Sample Surveys," *American Sociological Review* 23 (June 1958): 284–94.
16. Schattschneider, p. 35.
17. Lawrence D. Longley, "Interest Group Interactions in a Legislative System," *Journal of Politics* 29 (August 1967): 637–58.
18. Presthus, pp. 197, 425. Others have found that groups considered powerful are not necessarily the only groups which influence policy making. See Wayne L. Francis, *Legislative Issues in the Fifty States: A Comparative Analysis* (Chicago: Rand McNally, 1967), p. 42.
19. Presthus, p. 196.
20. John W. Kingdon, *Congressmen's Voting Decisions* (New York: Harper & Row, 1973).
21. Presthus, pp. 206–30.
22. Ibid. Presthus found that attempts to inform legislators about constituency opinion were less effective because this was an area where most representatives felt they had little to learn.
23. See Milbrath, *The Washington Lobbyists;* and Donald R. Hall,

Cooperative Lobbying—The Power of Pressure (Tucson: University of Arizona Press, 1969).

24. Kingdon, p. 142.
25. Arnold M. Rose, "Voluntary Associations under Conditions of Competition and Conflict," *Social Forces* 34 (December 1955): 159–63.
26. Two major studies using this model are: James S. Coleman, *Community Conflict* (New York: Free Press, 1957), and Robert L. Crain et al., *The Politics of Community Conflict: The Fluoridation Decision* (Indianapolis: Bobbs-Merrill, 1969).
27. Coleman, p. 24.
28. "It is characteristic of large numbers of people in our society that they see and think in terms of stereotypes, personalization, and over-simplifications, that they cannot recognize or tolerate ambiguous situations, and that they accordingly respond chiefly to symbols that over-simplify and distort." Murray Edelman, *The Symbolic Uses of Politics* (Urbana: University of Illinois Press, 1964), p. 31.
29. Thus fluoridation becomes an issue not of health but of governmental intrusion on individual rights; gun control is redefined as an issue involving the Second Amendment and the rights of sportsmen rather than of crime control.
30. Cobb and Elder, pp. 96–122.
31. Bachrach and Baratz define nondecision making as a "process by which the demands for change . . . can be suffocated before they are even voiced . . . or killed before they gain access to the relevant decision making arena." This is distinguishable from genuine (albeit negative) decisions such as deciding not to act or deciding not to decide. See Peter Bachrach and Morton S. Baratz, *Power and Poverty* (New York: Oxford University Press, 1970, p. 44.

2 An Amendment above Suspicion?

Despite the controversy surrounding the Equal Rights Amendment after its submission to the states, it was by no means a new policy, hastily conceived and passed by Congress without due deliberation. To the contrary, it had had a lengthy legislative history, which furnished several documents clearly stating the intent of Congress in approving it. Nor did it represent any departure from the general public policies and prevailing opinions of the period, 1963–72. Thus, ERA passage is viewed here as the culmination of a prolonged conflict within Congress and among this country's major interest groups—a conflict which ended in an impressive consensus in support of the ERA, buttressed to no small degree by the emergence of a new feminist movement.

Legal Interpretation and Legislative Intent

The Senate and House Joint Resolution containing the proposed Equal Rights Amendment provides as follows:

> Resolved by the Senate and House of Representatives of the United States of America in Congress assembled (two-thirds of each House concurring therein), That the following article is proposed as an amendment to the Constitution of the United

31

States, which shall be valid to all intents and purposes as part of the Constitution when ratified by the legislatures of three-fourths of the several States within seven years from the date of its submission by the Congress:

SECTION 1   Equality of rights under the law shall not be denied or abridged by the United States or by any State on account of sex.

SECTION 2   The Congress shall have the power to enforce, by appropriate legislation, the provisions of this article.

SECTION 3   This amendment shall take effect two years after the date of ratification.

Just as the Fifth and Fourteenth Amendments, which guarantee due process and equal protection, are couched in broad language, the ERA, too, contains such latitude. It is acknowledged that not every possible legal consequence can be foreseen prior to ratification. Because of this measure of uncertainty concerning its eventual interpretation by the courts, amendment opponents have cited authorities who foretell the ERA's legal effects very differently than do those whose views were adopted by a majority in Congress. Although the opposition gives the impression that all these authorities' views have equal weight and thus the legal impact of the ERA is largely unknown, this position is somewhat misleading. The courts, when interpreting amendments to the Constitution, traditionally consider the intent and purpose of the Congress in proposing and of the state legislatures in ratifying the amendments.[1]

In determining legislative intent, the courts will rely primarily upon the floor debate in both houses of Congress and the Senate Judiciary Committee report.[2] Both houses of Congress overwhelmingly passed the same version of the joint resolution; a conference committee to resolve differences between the two houses was not needed. The chief supporters were in remarkably close agreement concerning its impact, as expressed in the Senate Judiciary Committee majority report and in the floor debate.[3] The courts will also be interested in a 1971 *Yale Law Journal* article written to provide a comprehensive theory of the ERA.[4] This article was distributed by Congresswoman Martha Griffiths (D.-Mich.), chief sponsor in the House, to all members of the House and was inserted in the *Congressional Record* by Senator Birch Bayh (D.-Ind.), chairperson of the Senate Subcommittee on Constitutional Amendments. One of the most persuasive witnesses during both the House and Senate hearings was one of the article's coauthors, Yale Law School Professor Thomas Emerson. His statements were incorporated into those of the proponents in both houses.[5]

Because the controversy over the ERA has raged foremost around varying interpretations of its legal implications, those parts of the Senate Judiciary Committee majority report and the congressional floor debate dealing with the anticipated effects of the ERA upon several aspects of American life are of particular importance. No claim is made here that these constitute the amendment's "correct" interpretation. However, in the light of previous court practice in interpreting constitutional amendments, they represent a reasonable one.[6]

Education

With respect to education, Congress intended that schools at all levels that are publicly supported eliminate laws or regulations or official practices discriminating between males and females, including the sex segregation of schools and colleges, facilities, and instructional programs. Decisions regarding admissions and distribution of financial aid would be based upon merit or other pertinent considerations, not on the basis of gender. Policies involving employment and promotion in schools also would have to be unequivocally free from sex discrimination.[7]

Less clear is the potential effect of the ERA upon school athletics. Under Title IX of the Education Amendments Act of 1972, exceptional male and female athletes now compete against one another in some sports. Although there are many possible routes to equality of athletic education and competition for both sexes, the precise method of implementation cannot be predicted.[8]

Criminal Law

The amendment was expected to prohibit a state from providing for different statutory or administrative policies in sentencing and parole for males and females who commit the same crime. But the amendment should not invalidate laws punishing forcible rape, for such laws are designed to protect women in regard to ways in which they are uniformly distinct from men.[9]

Military Service

It was intended that women be allowed to volunteer for military service on the same basis as do men. It is likely that both men and women who meet the physical and other requirements, and who are not exempt or deferred by law, would be subject to conscription, if a draft law is in force, and would be assigned to various duties (including combat) depending on their qualifications and the service's needs. Women in the military would receive the same benefits as do men, including preferential treatment in federal and many state civil service appointments, medical care, and educational skills learned in the service or through the GI Bill. Responding to fears that mothers would be taken from their children into military service under the ERA, supporters in Congress noted that Congress would retain ample power to create legitimate sex-neutral exemptions from compulsory service (e.g., exempting both male and female *parents* with children under eighteen years of age).[10]

Domestic Relations

State domestic relations laws would have to be based on individual circumstances and needs and not on sexual stereotypes. It was not intended that both a husband and wife be required to contribute identical amounts of money to a marriage. The support obligation of each spouse could be defined in functional terms based, for example, on each spouse's earning power, current resources, and nonmonetary contributions to the family welfare. Where one spouse is the primary wage earner and the other runs the home, the wage earner might have the duty to support the spouse who stays at home in compensation for the performance of her or his household duties. Sex-neutral alimony and child support laws could also be drafted to take into consideration the spouse who had hitherto remained outside the labor force in order to perform domestic tasks or child care or both. Similarly, laws regarding child custody could be written that are based on the child's welfare and sex-neutral concepts of parental care.[11]

Homosexual Marriages

When it was suggested during the Senate floor debate that the ERA might prevent a state from prohibiting marriages between men partners or between women partners, the idea was sharply rejected by the amendment's supporters. The ERA would require only uniformity, that is, if a state legislature makes a judgment that it is illegal for a man to marry a man, then it must also be illegal for a woman to marry a woman, or vice versa.[12]

Privacy

The ERA was not meant to prohibit the states from requiring a reasonable separation of persons of different sexes under certain circumstances. The constitutional right of privacy established by the Supreme Court and the traditional power of the state to regulate cohabitation and sexual activity by unmarried persons would [still] permit the state to require segregation of the sexes with respect to such facilities as sleeping quarters at coeducational colleges, prison dormitories, and military barracks. Likewise, a separation of the sexes with respect to such places as public toilets would be possible.[13] The right to privacy could [still be] maintained within a sex-integrated prison, college dormitory, or military barracks, should these be mandated by the principle of sex equality under the ERA.[14]

Labor Legislation

The ERA was intended to assure equal treatment for men and women with regard to state labor laws. Labor laws barring women entirely from occupations where sex is not a "bona fide occupational qualification" (e.g., actress or wet-nurse) would be invalid. It was expected that restrictive laws which do not take into account the capacities, preferences, and abilities of individual females (such as weight lifting laws and limitations on hours of work) would become null and void. But those laws conferring a real benefit (e.g., rest periods, minimum wage, health and safety requirements) would, it was foreseen, be extended to protect both men and women.[15] In practice, Title VII of the Civil Rights Act of 1964 has already brought many such changes. The ERA would provide only an additional mandate for conformity to the principles of Title VII and extend Title VII's protection to employers with fewer than fifteen employees.[16]

States' Rights

The language of Section 2 of the ERA has also been the source of much controversy. It reads: "The Congress shall have the power to enforce, by appropriate legislation, the provisions of this article." The deletion of the words "and the several states [shall have the power] within their respective jurisdictions," which appeared in the resolutions considered in the 91st Congress (1969–70), from the resolution passed in the 92nd Congress (1971–72) has been interpreted by opponents as having taken enforcement power away from the state legislatures and placed it exclusively in the federal courts. An examination of legislative history, however, indicates that this wording is that of the customary enforcement clause, taken from Section 5 of the Fourteenth Amendment. Almost identical language is also found in the Thirteenth, Fifteenth, Nineteenth, Twenty-third, Twenty-fourth, and Twenty-sixth Amendments.[17] The change in language was made because of objections to the original unconventional language by constitutional authorities, who pointed out that this would be "a more restrictive authorization to Congress than is to be found in any other amendment."[18] Under the federal system of the United States, power to act and enforce any constitutional amendment lies with both the federal government and the states. That the deletion of the phrase "and the several states" would in no way weaken or deny the right of the states to legislate in compliance with the ERA was specified during floor debate in the House.[19] Section 2, as it stands, makes it clear that Congress also has the power to enforce the amendment by appropriate legislation.

The Congress specifically assigned the state legislatures the primary responsibility for revising any state laws conflicting with the ERA. The reason for delaying the amendment's effective date for two years after ratification, as provided in Section 3, was to allow state legislatures and agencies an opportunity to review and revise their sex-discrimination laws and regulations.[20] The federal courts, it was expected, would be involved in interpreting the amendment only in those cases where citizens believed that the Congress or the states had not amended their laws or official practices to conform.

An Unnecessary Amendment

Another opposition argument is that the Fourteenth Amendment, which guarantees "equal protection of the laws," suffices for constitutional redress of sex discrimination. Again, the congressional majority appears to have strongly disagreed.[21] The Senate report discusses a number of legal areas where discrimination against women still exists and concludes by pointing to the refusal of the Supreme Court in *Reed v. Reed*, 401 U.S. 71 (1971), to declare that discrimination based on sex, like that based on race, is inherently "suspect" and cannot be justified in the absence of a "compelling and overriding state interest." In recent years, the Court has upheld several laws discriminating between men and women.[22] Congress also rejected the argument that sex discrimination could be eliminated through statutory revision and case-by-case litigation without resort to a constitutional amendment. Without the legal impetus of the ERA, Congress felt, the process would be far too haphazard and slow.[23]

Legislative History

An equal rights amendment was first introduced in Congress in 1923, three years after ratification of the Nineteenth (Women's Suffrage) Amendment, with Representative Daniel Anthony (R.-Kans.), a nephew of Susan B. Anthony, as one of its sponsors. It read: "Men and women shall have equal rights throughout the United States and every place subject to its jurisdiction." Constitutional amendments with similar or identical wording were introduced in nearly every Congress from 1923 to the date of final passage in 1972.[24]

A number of hearings on the proposed amendment were held in the Senate during this period and it was always approved by the committee. In the 81st (1950) and 83rd (1953) Congresses, the ERA passed the Senate, although with a floor amendment attached. The latter, known as the "Hayden rider," after its author, Senator Carl Hayden (D.-Ariz.), stipulated that the amendment "shall not be construed to impair any rights, benefits, or exemptions now or hereafter conferred by law upon members of the female sex." The intent was to retain all state laws providing special benefits for women in employment. And in the 86th Congress (1959–60), the resolution's Senate sponsors withdrew it when the Hayden rider was again added on the floor. During the entire period that the amendment was before Congress, the House was consistently less active on the ERA. The House Judiciary Committee held hearings once in 1948, but none again until 1971, owing to the refusal of the Chairman, Representative Emanuel D. Celler (D.-N.Y.), to schedule them.[25]

The pivotal year in the ERA's legislative history was 1970. In May, the Senate Subcommittee on Constitutional Amendments held the first hearings since 1956 on the matter. A number of legislators testified, as did the leaders of nearly every national women's organization and many prominent lawyers; of the 42 witnesses heard, most supported the amendment.

For the first time in years, the ERA was also being considered in the House. On June 11, Representative Martha Griffiths (D.-Mich.), an active and longtime supporter of women's rights, was successful in her move to force the amendment out of the House Judiciary Committee by use of a discharge petition. It was brought onto the floor for a vote on August 10, where, after an hour's debate, it was overwhelmingly passed, 350 to 15.

The House-passed resolution was not referred to a committee at the request of the Senate leadership, and on October 6,

1970, it came before the Senate. After several days of debate, on October 13, 1970, the Senate adopted, 36 to 33, a provision exempting women from the draft. After the introduction of several unrelated riders[26] the ERA was laid aside and no further action was taken in the 91st Congress. Ironically, 80 senators—more than the two-thirds required for passage— were listed as sponsors of the amendment as introduced in that Congress. Inevitably, there was speculation among pro-ERA forces that many senators had lent their names only because they felt confident that House passage would be impossible, given the opposition of House Judiciary Committee Chairman Emanuel Celler.

The amendment was again introduced in the 92nd Congress in both houses and hearings were held by a House Subcommittee on the Judiciary in March 1971. The full House Judiciary Committee reported it out favorably with the addition of a provision that it would "not impair the validity of any law of the United States which exempts a person from compulsory military service or any other law of the United States or any state which reasonably promotes the health and safety of the people." On October 12, 1971, this committee amendment was rejected in the House, 104 to 254, and the ERA, as introduced, was approved, 354 to 23.

On November 22, 1971, the Senate Subcommittee on Constitutional Amendments adopted substitute language for the House Joint Resolution on the ERA and the Senate versions of the same resolution. As reported to the full Judiciary Committee, the amendment now included a section stipulating that "Neither the United States nor any state shall make any legal distinction between the rights and responsibilities of male and female persons unless such distinction is based on physiological or functional differences between them." In the full committee meeting on February 29, 1972, it was decided by a vote of 15 to 1 to reject the subcommittee's language and to report the joint resolution on the ERA, as introduced, favorably to the floor. Also defeated were attempts to include sections explicitly related to the draft, military service, child support, protective labor legislation, sex crimes, privacy, and the admissions policies of institutions of higher education. On March 22, 1972, the Senate approved the unamended version of the ERA by a vote of 84 to 8. Although a number of floor amendments, similar to those defeated in committee, were proposed during the extensive debate, the greatest number of votes any single one of them received was 18.

The Development of a Constituency for the ERA

This overwhelming congressional support for the ERA (and the equally strong rejection of crippling amendments) did not arise in a sociopolitical vacuum. The feeling in the Congress was widespread that, after almost fifty years of intermittent debate and long periods of neglect, the ERA embodied an important and timely principle. Concurrent with the re-surgence of a strong feminist movement in the late 1960s, a near consensus among women's organizations and other major interest groups developed on the need for the Equal Rights Amendment in order to eliminate the most prevalent form of discrimination in the American legal system. Public opinion was also moving in this direction, with the current surveys showing increasingly higher levels of public aware-ness of sex discrimination and greater acceptance of a more important role for women in public life and in the economy. Passage of the ERA was also consistent with the general trend of state and federal legislation and court decisions over the preceding decade.

The Early Conflict over the ERA

Although Congress, in passing the ERA, was acting in re-sponse to public demands in 1972, the Equal Rights Amend-ment had earlier been a major source of conflict among estab-lished interest groups. It had been proposed in 1923 by the National Woman's Party, the militant wing of the recently successful suffrage movement, and was immediately opposed by the other wing of that movement, the League of Women Voters (formerly the National American Woman Suffrage As-sociation).[27] Gradually, other interest groups came to endorse the amendment. Ironically, the League of Women Voters was the last major women's group to do so, in May 1972, shortly after congressional passage. (Only the AFL–CIO, among major national interest organizations, was slower to accept the amendment, and did not formally announce its support until October 1973, after several state councils and affiliated unions had broken rank to align themselves with the ERA.)

The conflict between the groups over the amendment stemmed from both philosophical differences concerning goals and tactics and a basic disagreement over the desirability of existing protective labor legislation. The National Woman's Party (NWP) focused solely upon the goal of total equality for women. Rather than approach that objective through piecemeal legislation, they favored a constitutional amendment ending all legal distinctions between men and women. The League of Women Voters, in alliance with other reform groups and labor unions, addressed itself to a variety of issues, not all of which were connected to women's rights. The League, in fact, has traditionally avoided being identified with women's rights per se, preferring to be known as an organization concerned with the entire community. Further, it adopted a strategy of gradualism for the advancement of women in society. Its members were proud of having secured passage of minimum-wage and maximum-hour laws for women and feared that the ERA would eliminate those statutes singling out women for special benefits in employment. Whatever the future conditions of employment might be, they believed, women currently needed to be protected by special laws concerning employment.

Because ERA supporters were willing to risk sacrificing this protective legislation to the broad aim of female equality, the charge was made that the amendment was an issue supported only by women of property, the professions, and business.[28] It is true that the only supporters of the ERA for many years were the NWP, composed of wealthy, educated women in late middle age; the National Federation of Business and Professional Women's Clubs (endorsed the ERA in 1937); and the General Federation of Women's Clubs (endorsed the ERA in 1944). ERA opponents were members of organizations representing, for the most part, middle-class women, who were still supportive of protective legislation and special privileges for women. As late as 1968, the list of organizations still in opposition included: the Women's Bureau of the Department of Labor, the American Association of University Women, the

League of Women Voters, the National Board of the Young Women's Christian Association, the National Council of Catholic Women, the American Civil Liberties Union, and the trade unions.[29] With the exception of the National Council of Catholic Women, which has remained in opposition, all these groups had come to support the ERA by the end of 1973.

Support within the executive branch of the federal government and the national political parties was also increasing. In 1940, the Republican platform had included an endorsement of the ERA and in 1944 the Democrats followed suit. Not until the 1960s were planks on the ERA dropped from the national party platforms, possibly in reaction to the conclusion reached by the Commission on the Status of Women, established by President Kennedy in 1961, that the amendment was not now necessary. However, both the Citizens' Advisory Council on the Status of Women, created by President Kennedy in 1963, and the President's Task Force on Women's Rights and Responsibilities, created by President Nixon in 1969, strongly advocated the ERA. It also had received the approval of Presidents Truman, Eisenhower, Kennedy, Johnson, and Nixon. For the first time in its history, in 1970 the Department of Labor supported the ERA. And both political parties again urged its ratification in 1972.

Finally, the balance of legal opinion in the 1970s favored the passage of the Equal Rights Amendment. This is evidenced by the formal endorsements of various bar associations and other legal groups, as well as by the preponderance of favorable legal testimony offered in the congressional hearings. Of those who testified in opposition, several believed that women were already adequately covered by the Fourteenth Amendment and that the courts would eventually apply that amendment to discrimination based on sex with the same vigor as to distinctions based on race. Therefore, in their view, the ERA was superfluous.

Public Policy on the Status of Women

The general trend of state and federal policy and court decisions in the area of sex discrimination over the period 1961–72 was undoubtedly important in breaking down resistance to the ERA, particularly among the labor unions and social reform groups. Interest was renewed in formulating and implementing a national policy for the improvement of the status of women, growing out of and with the movement for equality for minorities.

By 1972, a number of federal programs designed to end sex discrimination in employment were in effect.[30] The Equal Pay Act, the first of these, was signed on June 10, 1963. It required that male and female workers covered by the Fair Labor Standards Act (about 60 percent of all wage and salary earners) receive equal pay for equal work performed under equal conditions. Although the law permits differentials in pay based on a seniority or merit system, or any other factor aside from gender, a major omission was corrected in July 1972 when executive, administrative, and professional workers were brought under its coverage. Title VII, the Equal Employment Opportunity section of the Civil Rights Act of 1964, prohibits discrimination based on race, color, religion, national origin, or gender by private employers, employment agencies, unions, and state and local governments. The only important exception is employers with fewer than 15 employees. Two executive orders also addressed sex discrimination in employment: E. O. 11246 (as amended by E.O. 11375, October 1967), requiring that federal contractors not discriminate, and E.O. 11478 (August 1969), forbidding discrimination by the federal government and obliging all its agencies and departments to set up affirmative action programs.

The problem of sex discrimination in education was also considered by the 92nd Congress. By Title IX of the Education Amendments Act of 1972, any school—from the preschool level through graduate institutions—that receives federal funds is prohibited from discriminating on the basis of sex. Other laws equalizing employment and retirement benefits were passed by that Congress and several other bills related to women were given serious consideration.[31]

Furthermore, since 1963 most states had passed one or more laws forbidding sex discrimination in employment, often modeled upon the federal laws. There were several state statutes barring sex discrimination in public accommodations, housing, credit, and education.[32] In 1970–71, three states—Illinois, Pennsylvania, and Virginia—had adopted constitutional provisions similar to the federal ERA.

Presidents have commonly responded to the challenges of specific problems or groups by appointing commissions and task forces.[33] The specific recommendations of three such bodies formed to study the problems of women in America reflect a striking evolution toward support for a broad-based and effective attack on the traditionally secondary social and legal status of women. The President's Commission on the Status of Women (1961) was the first official body ever to examine the status of women in the United States. In general, its report, *American Women*, was moderate in its recommendations and consisted primarily of compilations of data. It endorsed the concept of protective labor legislation and argued that women's legal rights were already protected by the Fifth and Fourteenth Amendments, making the ERA unnecessary.[34] But even though it clearly assigned to women a unique role in society as wife and mother, it also urged many prevailing feminist goals such as day care services, reform of social security regulations, appointment of women to policy positions in government, and nondiscrimination by federal contractors. Several of the Commission's suggestions were immediately enacted. But perhaps more important, this first commission gave birth to the U.S. Citizens' Advisory Council on the Status of Women (1963) and to the state commissions on the status of women which were active in almost all states by 1972.

The Citizens' Advisory Council, composed of 20 private citizens appointed by the President, has proven to be a forerunner in the women's rights movement. In addition to sponsoring conferences bringing together women from the state commissions and a vigorous publications program on the subject of the status of women, the Council has strongly advocated a broad interpretation of the Title VII provisions, liberalized abortion, domestic support laws based on ability to pay, passage of the ERA, and the treatment of pregnancy as a temporary disability in employment. Likewise, the President's Task Force on Women's Rights and Responsibilities, set up by Nixon in October 1969 to provide ideas for his 1970

State of the Union address, issued a strong report in 1970 which was widely noted due to its unusually militant tone.[35]

Party platforms in 1972 also reflected a keen awareness of policies needed to bring women into the mainstream of American life. Beyond an endorsement of the ERA, the Republican platform contained eight items specifically related to the rights of women, including a call for the elimination of discrimination in credit, in government employment, and in the administration of criminal justice. The Democrats, too, went on record in favor of these policies and further urged stronger powers of enforcement for the Equal Employment Opportunity Commission (EEOC) and extension of the equal pay laws to all workers, including domestics.

The courts, as well, were beginning to move against sex discrimination, although sex, unlike race, color, creed, national origin, or religion, was still accepted as a legitimate classification. The Supreme Court for the first time in 1971 invalidated a state law discriminating against women. Involved was an Idaho law giving preference to men over women as administrators of estates.[36] There was also evident a strong court trend toward the invalidation under Title VII of state protective legislation—such as maximum-hour and weight limitations—which clearly discriminated against women. State after state had voluntarily amended protective labor laws by the 1970s to bring them into compliance with federal equal opportunity legislation.

The Feminist Movement, Women's Rights, and American Interest Groups

The reemergence of a strong and visible feminist movement in the United States, dating from the late 1960s, also played a major role in generating support for the ERA among interest groups, public officials, and the public at large. Social movements are commonly viewed as responses to societal strain and change. And the decade of the 1960s had seen many challenges to the American political system to fulfill its traditional promises: the student protests, the antiwar movement, the demonstrations at the 1968 Chicago Democratic National Convention, and the civil rights movement.[37] But social ferment does not in itself create social movements; it only creates the potential for such movements.

Whether social movements are more likely to form during periods when potential activists are experiencing their worst periods of deprivation or when they are gaining increasing status is unclear. Examples can be cited to support both views. The black civil rights movement, for example, came after a significant rise in the income and education levels of blacks. Similarly, among women in the 1960s, the number of those receiving college and advanced degrees was rising rapidly, even though the number of degrees earned by women in 1970, as a percentage of all such degrees conferred that year, was roughly equivalent to that in 1930 (see table 2.1). Women's participation in the labor force was also steadily rising (see table 2.2). Job opportunities, a declining birthrate,

Table 2.1
Female Educational Attainment, 1890–1975

Year	Degrees Awarded to Women as a Percentage of the Total Degrees		
	B.A.	M.A.	Ph.D.
1890	17	19	1
1900	19	19	6
1910	23	26	10
1920	34	30	15
1930	40	40	15
1940	41	38	13
1950	24	29	10
1960	35	35	11
1970	42	40	13
1975	45	45	21

Sources: U.S. Department of Labor, Women's Bureau, *1969 Handbook on Women Workers* (Washington, D.C.: Government Printing Office, 1969), p. 191; Rudolf Blitz, "Women in the Professions," *Monthly Labor Review* 97 (May 1974), p. 38; U.S. National Center for Education Statistics, *Earned Degrees Conferred 1974–75* (Washington, D.C.: Government Printing Office, 1977), p. 10.

TABLE 2.2
Female Labor Force Participation, 1940–75

Year	Percent of Total Labor Force	Percent of All Women	Percent of Married Women, Husband Present
1940	25	29	15
1950	29	33	24
1960	33	37	31
1970	38	43	41
1975	40	46	44

SOURCES: U.S. Department of Labor, Women's Bureau, *1975 Handbook on Women Workers* (Washington, D.C.: Government Printing Office, 1975), pp. 11, 18; U.S. Department of Labor, Women's Bureau, *Women Workers Today* (Washington, D.C.: Government Printing Office, 1976), pp. 1–3.

and a consumer-oriented society helped to transform the female labor force from one of primarily young single women to one of married women and mothers over 40.

Reference to the status of all American women may be less pertinent to the origins of the new feminist movement, however, than is the status of a particular part of that population. As Gusfield has noted:

> . . . social movements draw their adherents from particular segments of the society, people whose experiences make them more receptive to a particular ideology than others, whose conditions of life make communication and organization more possible, or who experience events in sharper and more intense form.[38]

That segment, in the case of the women's movement, would be middle-class, college-educated women, a group that may have had lower levels of absolute deprivation but whose sense of relative deprivation was significantly increasing.[39]

This group of women was more likely to adopt as their reference group, for purposes of comparison, men of similar educational backgrounds rather than members of their own sex. And as table 2.3 shows, the gap between the median incomes of women and men actually increases with educational

level. Furthermore, the earnings gap had become wider between 1955 and 1974 (see table 2.4). Finally, not only was the
average income of working women much lower than that of
white men, but even the income of nonwhite men exceeded
that of women (see table 2.5).

But despite the turmoil of the 1960s and the potential
awareness of relative deprivation among middle-class,
college-educated women, there was no significant change in
the status of such women which alone can account for the
growth of the new feminist movement at the particular time
at which this occurred. Rather, a series of events, preexisting
ideologies, and personal relationships combined to facilitate
the formation of a women's movement at this time.[40]

The founding of the National Organization for Women
(NOW) at the Third National Conference of State Commissions on the Status of Women, June 28–29, 1966, marked the
beginning of a new era in the women's rights movement.
NOW was the first of several new activist feminist groups
formed in the late 1960s and early 1970s to combat sex discrimination in all spheres of American life—social, political,
economic, and psychological. The Women's Equity Action
League (WEAL, 1968) and the National Women's Political

TABLE 2.3
Median Income for Male and Female Workers, by Education, 1974

(Full-time, Year-round Workers)

Educational Level	Women's Median Wage	Men's Median Wage	Difference
Less than 8 years elementary	$5,002	$ 7,912	$2,890
8 years elementary	5,606	9,891	4,285
4 years high school	7,150	12,642	5,492
4 years college	9,523	16,240	6,717

SOURCE: U.S. Department of Labor, Women's Bureau, *The Earnings Gap Between Women and Men* (Washington, D.C.: Government Printing Office, 1976), p. 10.

TABLE 2.4
Median Income for Women as a Percentage
of Median Income for Men, 1955–74

Year	Percent
1955	64
1960	61
1965	60
1970	59
1974	57

SOURCE: U.S. Department of Labor, Women's Bureau, *The Earnings Gap Between Women and Men* (Washington, D.C.: Government Printing Office, 1976), p. 6.

Caucus (NWPC, 1971) are the other principal new feminist groups with a strong national headquarters and a membership base organized into state and local units.[41]

The emergence of these new women's rights groups placed certain severe pressures upon older organizations such as the League of Women Voters (LWV), the American Association of University Women (AAUW), and the Young Women's Christian Association (YWCA). A great deal of hesitancy was expressed among these, including that longtime ERA supporter, the Business and Professional Women's Clubs (BPW), to become identified with the fight against sex discrimination for fear of being labeled "feminist" and "militant."[42] In a story prepared to coincide with the August 26, 1970, Women's Strike for Equality (the largest demonstration for women's equality in U.S. history), a *New York Times* reporter surveyed leaders of several of these traditional women's organizations. She found apprehension among some that their groups would deteriorate into worthless anachronisms and would ultimately pass from existence. Only the AAUW representative expressed hope that traditional groups would adopt a spirit of activism and militancy in order to remain timely and viable.[43]

The argument has been made that the media have co-opted the women's movement into respectability by stressing its

TABLE 2.5
Average Salaries Earned by Working Men and Women, 1974

Workers (Full-time)	Average Salary
White men	$12,104
Nonwhite men	8,524
White women	6,823
Nonwhite women	6,258

SOURCE: U.S. Department of Commerce, Census Bureau, *Current Population Report* (1976), Bulletin P-60, no. 101, table 67.

more conservative features (equal pay and employment) and omitting its more radical aspects.[44] Yet traditional women's groups clearly underwent enough consciousness-raising concerning sexism during the sixties that by the seventies, perhaps as a result of the "relative deprivation" experienced by their predominantly middle-class, college-educated membership, they were ready to take positive steps to end it.

For example, the YWCA, an organization seldom actively involved in agitation for social change since its formation in 1867, issued this statement at its 1970 convention: "It is essential that women move beyond being sexual playthings of the male to an affirmation of their role as human beings, with capacity for leadership and contribution in varied ways. . . . They need an identity of their own."[45] The AAUW, too, has recognized the changing roles of women with the addition of a task force: Women in Transition. (The AAUW endorsed the ERA at its June 1971 convention.) And the League of Women Voters, at its 30th National Convention in May 1972 adopted a new wording of its Human Resources agenda item to include "support of equal rights for all regardless of race or *sex*" (my emphasis). Although the League usually studies an issue for one to two years before adding it to its legislative agenda, the convention, pointing to the new wording, authorized immediate action at the state and local levels on discriminatory practices against women and for the first time urged support of the ERA.

The new feminist movement also garnered acceptance from other types of interest groups. Women in trade unions, by the early seventies, had filed numerous suits under Title VII against their employers and even their own unions, often with the financial and legal assistance of NOW or WEAL. And, under pressure from their female membership, several unions endorsed the ERA (e.g., the United Auto Workers in April 1970; the Communication Workers of America in June 1972). Church groups which had formerly restricted their activities to volunteer social service projects also came to support female equality in the belief that sex discrimination had had an adverse effect upon American society. Many black organizations, particularly those composed of black women, acknowledged the linkages between sexism and racism and thus espoused the goals of the women's rights movement. Public interest organizations, too, adopted the women's movement issues as their own; particularly active have been Common Cause and Women's Rights Projects of the ACLU.

American Public Opinion and Women's Rights

While a diverse amalgamation of groups was coalescing around the subject of women's rights, an even more heterogeneous body, the American public, simultaneously was undergoing a process of consciousness-raising concerning sex discrimination and the desirable role of women in political life and society.

Public enthusiasm for the principle of equal pay for equal work has long enjoyed broad and steadily rising levels of support, ranging from 78 to 94 percent over the period 1942–77.[46] Nonetheless, the results of a questionnaire distributed in the April 1972 issue of *Redbook* magazine showed that of the more than 120,000 (female) readers who responded, 90 percent believed discrimination against women in pay and job opportunities was continuing.[47] Similarly, the 1972 Election Study conducted by the Survey Research Center of the University of Michigan found that almost 79 percent of the sample (men and women) saw continued sex discrimination in hiring policies.[48] This same survey showed that sexual stereotypes concerning ambition, reliability, and motherhood still are widely used as explanations for women's lower status. Regardless of this, almost 53 percent of the interviewees were willing to concur with the general indictment: "Our society discriminates against women."

Opinions concerning the appropriate role for women in society have undergone marked revisions. An early (1936) Gallup Poll found that 82 percent of the male/female sample flatly opposed a married woman's entering the labor force if her husband was capable of supporting her.[49] By 1974, the National Opinion Research Center (NORC) General Social Survey of males and females indicated that feelings had reversed and 68 percent now approved of working wives. The University of Michigan 1972 Election Study also found far greater sanction for working wives. In a situation where cutbacks in employment are necessary, almost 52 percent of the male/female sample thought male and female employees should be treated impartially. This same study also indicated that roughly 46 percent of the respondents agreed that women should have an equal role with men in society, as compared with about 29 percent who still adhered to the belief that women's place is in the home.[50]

The women's rights movement was attracting increased support as well (see table 2.6). When asked in 1970 whether they favored or opposed most of the efforts to strengthen and change women's status in contemporary society, women were

TABLE 2.6
Efforts to Strengthen or Change Women's Status
in Society, 1970–74

	1970		1972		1974	
	M	F	M	F	M	F
Favor	44%	40%	49%	48%	63%	57%
Oppose	39	42	36	36	19	25
Not sure	17	18	15	16	18	18

SOURCE: The Roper Organization, Inc., *The Virginia Slims American Women's Opinion Poll* (New York, 1974), vol. 3, p. 3.

almost equally divided. Four years later, women were decisively in favor of such attempts. Men were even more supportive of enhancing women's status.

Another aim of the women's rights movement is increased participation of women in politics, whether as elected or appointed officials, members of political parties or interest groups, or as partisans of the more amorphous "women's liberation movement." A traditional bellwether of public acceptance of women in politics has been expressed willingness to support a qualified female nominee of one's party for President. According to Gallup and NORC polls, such confidence has steadily mounted over the years from a low of 33 percent in 1945 to a high of 77 percent in 1974 (see figure 2.1). For lower elective offices, the level of expressed support for female candidates is even higher. Given the increasing number of women in public office, the gap between opinion and behavior may be minimal.[51]

In general, agreement is strong that women should be involved in politics. Only 19 percent of the 1972 Election Study sample concurred with the statement: "Women should stay out of politics." And the 1972 Louis Harris poll found that the majority of women (59%) and men (55%) believed women should become even more active politically. Less than 10 percent of either favored a reduced role for women.[52] Support was also expressed for increased female participation in the national party conventions, although most respondents were ambivalent about the desirability of proportional representation.[53]

Indications of public approval of women acting within political organizations in order to obtain equality for women vary according to the precise wording of the question. For example, when asked with which of these statements they agreed more, male/female respondents in the 1972 Election Study aligned themselves as follows:

55.5% **1.** Women can best overcome discrimination by pursuing their individual career goals in as feminine a way as possible.

40.7% **2.** It is not enough for a woman to be successful herself; women must work together to change laws and customs that are unfair to all women.

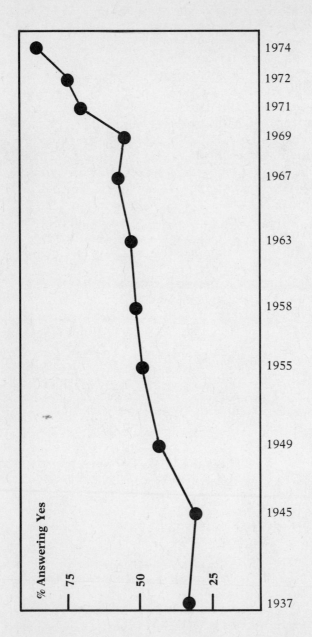

FIGURE 2.1

Willingness to Vote for Woman for President

SOURCES: *"The Gallup Poll: Public Opinion, 1935–1971"* (New York: Random House, 1972); National Opinion Research Center, *General Social Survey*, Spring 1974 (ICPR Study Number 7341).

75.4% **1.** The best way to handle problems of discrimination is for each woman to make sure she gets the best training possible for what she wants to do.

20.1% **2.** Only if women organize and work together can anything really be done about discrimination.

This breakdown would suggest that a sizable part of the population is hostile to women working together to combat sex discrimination. However, the same study also found that the influence of women's groups in American life and politics was considered "just about right" by about 47 percent of the sample, with those who felt women's groups have "too little" influence outnumbering those who felt they have "too much" by more than 4½ to 1. The traditional American predilection for individual initiative in surmounting difficulties seems to have been tapped in the earlier sets of questions.

There is also the problem of the pejorative connotations raised by the phrase "women's liberation." In the Louis Harris poll, a majority of women (52 percent) and men (54 percent) favored organizations to strengthen women's participation in politics. Only 29 percent of both sexes were opposed to such organizations. However, when the question was posed in terms of attitude toward the efforts of "women's liberation groups," only 39 percent of the women described themselves as "sympathetic," and fully 49 percent were "unsympathetic." (Men were evenly divided, 42 percent on each side.)[54] Yet, one-half of those women responding to the *Redbook* survey felt that the feminist movement had changed their thinking and made them more aware of sex discrimination, and two out of every three expressed their support of that movement.[55] The goals, organizations, and activities of the women's movement thus enjoyed impressive levels of affirmation. Only when the movement was identified by its popular name, "women's liberation," did it suffer a loss of public approbation.

In view of these conditions surrounding congressional passage of the ERA, rapid and decisive ratification in the states was predicted by most observers, as has been noted. The amendment was seemingly congruent with society's prevailing value system, as mirrored in public opinion surveys concerning the role of women. Furthermore, after a fifty-year period of study and debate, the ERA now reflected the values of the Congress. Although some members of Congress still felt grave misgivings about its impact, the vast majority were united in support of the amendment. Questions concerning military service, domestic relations, privacy, and protective legislation were raised and satisfactorily resolved in committee and floor debate. Crippling amendments fell far short of the majorities they had received in past sessions. Since the state legislatures are a major reservoir of recruitment to Congress, it was felt that the ERA was compatible with the outlook of these decision makers as well.

A strongly committed coalition of well-established and politically experienced organizations also affirmed the ERA, having resolved earlier conflicts. Conversely, few organizations had materialized in opposition, a situation which greatly strengthened the amendment's chances of success.

A final source of advocacy for the ERA was elite opinion. Several Presidents of the United States and the two major political parties had formally embraced it. Key bureaucracies, a Presidential Commission, and a Presidential Task Force commended it with positive research and well-disposed publications. Those with special expertise on the ERA—lawyers—supported it individually and through the American Bar Association. In short, it appeared that everyone who was "anyone" was in favor of the ERA.

Yet, the predicted rapid and decisive ratification of the ERA did not occur. In retrospect, this is even more intriguing, given: (1) the even stronger allegiance to women's rights shown by public opinion polls taken after 1972; (2) the large number of women elected to public office from 1972 to 1976; and (3) the continuing support in state legislatures for measures abolishing discrimination based on gender.

NOTES

1. For one attempt to place the debate over the ERA within the context of legislative intent, see U.S. Citizens' Advisory Council on the Status of Women, *Interpretation of the Equal Rights Amendment in Accordance with Legislative History* (Washington, D.C.: Government Printing Office, 1974).

2. U.S., Congress, Senate, *Equal Rights for Men and Women*, S. Rept. 92-689, 92d Cong., 2d sess., 1972, p. 2.
3. The majority report of the House Judiciary Committee, which endorsed the Wiggins amendment (exempting women from the draft and retaining protective labor legislation), was rejected in the full House, 265–87. Fourteen members of the House Judiciary Committee, however, supported the original amendment and expressed their understanding of the amendment in "Separate Views." These separate views were incorporated into the Senate Judiciary Committee report. The Senate report thus expresses the intent of the chief proponents on both the House and Senate Judiciary Committees.
4. Thomas I. Emerson et al., "The Equal Rights Amendment: A Constitutional Basis for Equal Rights for Women," *Yale Law Journal* 80 (April 1971): 871–985.
5. Senator Sam Ervin, a leading Senate opponent of the ERA, also incorporated certain parts of the *Yale Law Journal* article into his minority views, contained in the Senate Judiciary Committee report, in support of his objections to the amendment. For a critique of Senator Ervin's apparently highly selective and misleading use of certain phrases and parts of paragraphs of this article, see U.S. Citizens' Advisory Council on the Status of Women, *The Equal Rights Amendment–Senator Ervin's Minority Report and the Yale Law Journal* (Washington, D.C.: Government Printing Office, 1972).
6. Also see Barbara A. Brown et al., *Women's Rights and the Law: The Impact of the ERA on State Laws* (New York: Praeger, 1977) and California Commission on the Status of Women, *Impact ERA; Limitations and Possibilities* (Millbrae, Cal.: Les Femmes, 1976).
7. U.S. Senate, pp. 16–17.
8. See Brown et al., pp. 304–8.
9. U.S. Senate, p. 16.
10. Ibid., pp. 13–14.
11. Ibid., pp. 17–18; Brown et al., pp. 120–21, 188.
12. U.S., Congress, Senate, 92d Cong., 2d sess., 21 March 1972, *Congressional Record* 118: S4389.
13. U.S. Senate, *Equal Rights*, p. 12. See also pp. 14, 17 for statements on military and school dressingrooms, restrooms and sleeping facilities.
14. Brown et al., pp. 88–89.
15. U.S. Senate, pp. 14–16.
16. Brown et al., pp. 219–20.
17. U.S. Senate, p. 20.
18. U.S., Congress, Senate, Committee on the Judiciary, *Hearings before the Committee on the Judiciary on S.J. Res. 61 and S.J. Res. 231*, 91st Cong., 2d sess., p. 80, testimony of Professor Paul A. Freund, *Equal Rights, 1970*.
19. U.S., Congress, House, 92d Cong., 1st sess., 12 October 1971, *Congressional Record* 117: H9391.
20. U.S. Senate, *Equal Rights*, p. 15.
21. Ibid., pp. 6–10.

22. See *Geduldig* v. *Aiello*, 417 U.S. 484 (1974); *Williams* v. *McNair*, 316 F. Supp. 134 (D.-S.C. 1970), aff'd., 401 U.S. 951 (1971); *Forbush* v. *Wallace*, 341 F.Supp. 217 (M.D.-Ala. 1971), aff'd., 405 U.S. 970 (1972); *Kahn* v. *Shevin*, 42 U.S.L.W. 4591 (1974); *Ballard* v. *Schlesinger*, 43 U.S.L.W. 4158 (1975).

23. U.S. Senate, *Equal Rights*, p. 11.

24. The wording of the amendment was revised by the Senate Judiciary Committee in 1943 to its present form. The original language was much more comprehensive and probably would have had a greater impact on private business than the present wording does.

25. Emanuel Celler was defeated in 1972 by a young feminist, Elizabeth Holtzman (D.-N.Y.), who effectively used his opposition to the ERA in her campaign.

26. One had to do with prayer in public buildings and another with the jurisdiction of public schools.

27. See William H. Chafe, *The American Woman: Her Changing Social, Economic, and Political Role, 1920–1970* (New York: Oxford University Press, 1972), pp. 112–32. Chafe argues that the inability of women's groups to agree upon the ERA played an important role in the decline of feminism after 1920.

28. Arnold W. Green and Eleanor Melnick, "What Has Happened to the Feminist Movement?" in *Studies in Leadership: Leadership and Democratic Action*, ed. Alvin W. Gouldner (New York: Harper & Row, 1950). pp. 277–302.

29. Martin Gruberg, *Women in American Politics: An Assessment and Sourcebook* (Oshkosh, Wis.: Academic 1968), p. 101.

30. See Irene L. Murphy, *Public Policy on the Status of Women* (Lexington, Mass.: Heath, 1973).

31. Ibid., pp. 47–61. The procession of antisex discrimination laws and other legislation of interest to women has not slowed in more recent Congresses, despite the difficulties the ERA has encountered in the states. In the 93d Congress (1973–74) more than 1.5 million domestic service workers were brought under the coverage of the Fair Labor Standards Act. A provision of the Housing and Community Development Act of 1974 prohibited sex discrimination in carrying out community development programs and in making federally related mortgages. The Equal Credit Opportunity Act of 1974 prohibited discrimination in credit on the basis of sex or marital status. The 94th Congress established a rape control center and appropriated $6.3 million for the Women's Educational Equity Program, formed to develop nonsexist curricula and counseling and to conduct a study of sex discrimination in public education similar to the Coleman Report on race.

32. See Susan C. Ross, *The Rights of Women* (New York: Avon, 1973), Appendix Charts A and B for a list of these state laws.

33. E.g., Anthony M. Platt, ed., *Politics of Riot Commissions* (New York: Macmillan, 1971).

34. One interpretation is that the commission was created in order to

remove the ERA from active consideration during the Kennedy administration as a concession to organized labor. See Judith Hole and Ellen Levine, *Rebirth of Feminism* (New York: Quadrangle, 1971), pp. 18–24.

35. See Hole and Levine, pp. 48–52, for a discussion of the suppression of this report by the Nixon administration.
36. *Reed* v. *Reed*, 404 U.S. 71 (1971).
37. The parallelisms between the feminist movements and the black movements in America, both past and present, has often been noted. See Helen Mayer Hacker, "Women as a Minority Group," *Social Forces* 30 (October 1951): 60–69; Catherine Stimpson, "Thy Neighbor's Wife, Thy Neighbor's Servants: Women's Liberation and Black Civil Rights," in *Woman in Sexist Society*, ed. Vivian Gornick and Barbara K. Moran (New York: New American Library, 1972), pp. 622–57; Gunnar Myrdal, "A Parallel to the Negro Problem," in *An American Dilemma*, vol. 2 (New York: Harper & Row, 1944), Appendix 5. Although no causal relationship should be imputed between the new feminist movement and the earlier black civil rights movement, the central focus of both movements on equality *now* was certainly an important linkage.
38. Joseph R. Gusfield, ed., *Protest, Reform, and Revolt: A Reader in Social Movements* (New York: Wiley, 1970), pp. 10–11.
39. "Relative deprivation" is not defined in terms of an absolute level of status or wealth but in terms of what people have come to feel is their just due, usually as the result of a comparison with the status of some other group or person.
40. For a discussion of the origins of the women's movement, see Jo Freeman, *The Politics of Women's Liberation* (New York: Longman, 1975). Freeman cites four elements contributing to the emergence of the movement: "(1) the growth of a preexisting communications network which was (2) co-optable to the ideas of the new movement; (3) a series of crises that galvanized into action people involved in this network; and (4) subsequent organizing effort to weld the spontaneous groups together into a movement," ibid., p. 62.
41. The new feminist movement, broadly defined, contains all four types of social movements discussed in Gusfield, pp. 85–89. No attention will be given to the feminist communes (withdrawal movement), the revolutionary feminist organizations such as the Symbionese Liberation Army or the Weather Underground, or, except in passing, the protest-oriented radical feminists. Although all branches of the movement are composed of predominantly middle-class well-educated women, the focus here is on the fourth type, the reform organizations with their gradualist and legitimate status and commitment to seeking changes in institutions within the "rules of the game."
42. Hole and Levine, p. 82.
43. Lacey Fosburgh, "Traditional Groups Prefer to Ignore Women's Lib," *New York Times*, 26 August 1970, p. 14. See also Alice L. Beeman and

Shirley McCune, "Changing Styles: Women's Groups in the Seventies," *AAUW Journal* 64 (November 1970): 24–26.

44. See Monica B. Morris, "Newspapers and the New Feminists: Black Out as Social Control? " *Journalism Quarterly* 50 (Spring 1973): 37–42; and Monica B. Morris, "Public Definition of a Social Movement: Women's Liberation," *Sociology and Social Research* 57 (July 1973): 526–43.

45. Quoted in Hole and Levine, p. 103.

46. See the Gallup Poll for February 13, 1942, and June 5, 1954. *The Gallup Poll: Public Opinion, 1935–1971* (New York: Random House, 1972), pp. 322, 1240. Also see *Parade* magazine polls appearing in the September 26, 1971, and April 15, 1973, issues and the Associated Press–NBC News poll, *Austin American-Statesman*, 4 December 1977, p. A10.

47. Carol Tavris and Toby Jayaratne, "What 120,000 Young Women Can Tell You About Sex, Motherhood, Menstruation, Housework—and Men," *Redbook* 140 (January 1973): 67ff.

48. The exact wording: "Many qualified women can't get good jobs; men with the same skills have much less trouble." (Agree–Disagree)

49. *The Gallup Poll*, p. 39.

50. The exact wording: "Recently there has been a lot of talk about women's rights. Some people feel that women should have an equal role with men in running business, industry, and government. Others feel that women's place is in the home. Where would you place yourself on this [7-point] scale or haven't you thought much about this?" Nineteen percent of the sample placed themselves in the middle of the scale; the remaining 6 percent were unable to respond.

51. Even though the number of women elected to Congress only increased by 1 (to 16) in 1972, the number of females in state legislatures increased 28.2 percent, from 344 to 441. This trend was accelerated, 1974–1977. Until November 8, 1978, 20 women were in Congress and 703 women were serving in the state legislatures. In addition, Connecticut and Washington had female governors and three states—New York, Kentucky, and Mississippi—had female lieutenant governors.

52. Louis Harris and Associates, *The 1972 Virginia Slims American Women's Opinion Poll* (New York, 1972), p. 18.

53. Ibid., pp. 42–43. Roughly 40 percent of the sample felt that there had been too few female delegates in the past, but in a later question, only 32 percent of the women and 24 percent of the men supported a delegation composed of equal numbers of men and women.

54. Louis Harris and Associates, pp. 4, 21.

55. Tavris and Jayaratne.

3 The Group Basis of Conflict

As has been seen, when the ERA was sent to the states for ratification, there already existed a large reservoir of potentially active supporters in the states, as evidenced by the lengthy list of national organizations on record in its favor (see Appendix D). Although an intensive lobbying effort had been waged to push the amendment through Congress, it was believed that it would now be quickly ratified without need of any major allocation of resources on the part of national organizations. And the record of ERA ratification in 1972 seemed to reinforce this belief. Of the 32 state legislatures in session in 1972 after the date of submission, 21 ratified with a minimum of procedural delay. Only rarely was elaborate political strategy required to assure passage. (Solely in California did the ERA encounter major difficulties in 1972 before ratification.) Opposition in 1972 was most commonly voiced by members of established politically conservative groups and of Happiness of Womanhood (HOW).

In the early months of 1973, the sympathizers were admittedly caught by surprise by the emergence of effective ad hoc organizations of conservative, predominantly Republican women under the leadership of Phyllis Schlafly of Illinois. Confronted by these and by the continuing hostility of the national AFL–CIO, proponent groups became aware of the need to develop a ratification strategy and to invest major financial and political resources on its implementation.

Activity on the National Level for the ERA

Although the national offices of groups supporting the ERA have been more active than have those of groups opposing it, they have not organized a coordinated campaign for expediting ratification.

The ERA Ratification Council, an umbrella coalition of about 30 proponent groups, had been formed shortly after congressional passage, ostensibly to work for ratification in the states. However, as a spokesperson for one of the member-organizations vouchsafed, the Council was little more than a luncheon group of veterans of congressional passage, set up to "pat each other on the back" and exchange information of which most were already aware. Although one of its stated aims was to serve as a central clearinghouse for research and information concerning the ERA, as late as December 1973 the Council had no staff and no materials for distribution. Its budget for 1973 totaled only about $1,000.

In April 1973, the Council *had* appointed an "ERA Action Committee," composed of delegates from four member-organizations—the National Woman's Party, Common Cause, the League of Women Voters, and Business and Professional Women's Clubs—to formulate a national ratification strategy. In late May, this committee recommended a plan which would have avoided duplication of effort by allowing each member-organization to confine its activity to areas where it was most experienced and capable. The National Women's Political Caucus, for example, was to identify those legislators opposed to the ERA who could be defeated for reelection and run candidates against them. The National Organization for Women would analyze the records and political-economic alliances of legislative opponents to determine what groups or individuals might bring pressure on them to change their viewpoint. NOW members were also to see to it the subject of the ERA was raised wherever the legislator appeared while seeking reelection. The Common Cause research staff was to analyze opposition arguments and prepare rebuttals. The League of Women Voters was to train lobbyists, particularly in smaller urban areas, where its constituency is far stronger than that of other proponent groups. On paper, this groundplan was excellent. However, the feeling was general that the Ratification Council leadership no longer had any interest in playing a major role in national ratification efforts and so the "Action Committee" met only once more before disbanding.

In the summer of 1973, informal meetings between representatives of some proponent organizations were initiated, culminating in the formation of an "Operation Task Force" for promoting ratification in the remaining states. All the member-groups belonged to the Ratification Council, but were distinguished from most of their confederates by their readiness to commit substantial economic assistance to the ERA. The Task Force included the National Organization for Women; the National Women's Political Caucus; the League of Women Voters; Common Cause; the American Civil Liberties Union; the International Union of United Automobile, Aerospace, and Agricultural Implement Workers of America; the American Association of University Women; the International Union of Electrical, Radio, and Machine Workers; and the United Methodist Women. The total sum these groups spent in 1973–74 on ERA activities—including staff salaries, printed materials and mailings, travel expenses, and direct cash payments to state branches of their respective organizations—has been estimated at $200,000.[1]

By 1974, after all unratified state legislatures had adjourned, a more cohesive national ratification strategy was considered essential by many of these Task Force organizations if victory was to be gained. There was no precedent for an amendment being added to the Constitution after the ratification process had extended beyond four calendar years, and in several states the ERA would come up on the legislative agenda for the fourth straight year in 1975. Furthermore, a seven-year time limitation upon ratification had been adopted by Congress as a compromise with legislative opponents of the ERA. The specific seven-year period was chosen because, since 1917, this had been customary. (The first 18 amendments to the Constitution had no deadline.)

The National Federation of Business and Professional Women's Clubs (BPW), which had not participated in the Task Force, took the initiative in the fall of 1974 by hiring the prominent Republican consulting firm of Bailey, Deardourff, and Eyre to do a study of the 17 unratified states based on field research and to recommend strategies. The enthusiasm which met its report to the December 10, 1974, meeting of the ERA Ratification Council marked the emergence of a new phase in activities. It was advised that significant national funding be put into the 10 states where chances for ratification in 1975 were best. Even where ratification seemed less likely, some national support funds were to be provided to state coalitions. In all, a budget of $249,000 was proposed for 1975 ERA efforts. Bailey, Deardourff, and Eyre further suggested that a National Coordinating Office and a separate and quite sophisticated National ERA Press Center be instituted in Washington for coordination, support to the states, and fund raising. Finally, the report urged the establishment of a new ERA 1975 Fund, solicited directly from individuals and independent of existing organizations.

In 1975, with the report serving as an additional impetus, representatives of several major proponent groups began planning the formation of a new, more active coalition. Prospective staff members for the new association were interviewed in the fall, and by December, about 30 organizations had agreed to act together. In January 1976, ERAmerica opened an office in the Washington, D.C., headquarters of the National Education Association. Cochaired by prominent political party women Democrat Liz Carpenter and Republican Elly Peterson, it employs a small paid staff. As originally conceived, ERAmerica was to wage a nationwide campaign for ratification similar to a political campaign, with speakers, fund-raising, strategy sessions, pamphlets, and wheeling and dealing in smoke-filled rooms. To win ratification by March 1979, a budget of $1 million was projected. Although established proponent groups have contributed money and services to the coalition and ERAmerica itself has sponsored several successful fund-raising events, it has not had the resources to play the central role envisioned and by 1978 serves primarily as a steering committee and clearinghouse for information on the amendment.

All the above-mentioned efforts at intergroup cooperation provided some degree of coordination among those national organizations actively in support of the ERA. At the same time, by virtue of these coalitions' looseness, individual member-groups have been free to pursue separate tactics in working for ratification.

The most ambitious fund-raising effort has been that of the Business and Professional Women's Clubs (BPW), which in the period of one year, 1973–74, raised $251,091 by assessing each club $2 per member. This money was used for direct grants to state ERA coalitions and state BPW groups and for materials and services provided by the national headquarters.

The League of Women Voters also has an ERA fund in excess of $100,000, acquired primarily through the sale of bracelets and special membership assessments. This money is allocated to the state chapters in all unratified states upon submission of a budget. The main functions of the national office are to coordinate state efforts, provide resource people and materials, and share information gleaned from other states or organizations.

The National Organization for Women is a third organization with a national ERA fund over $100,000. NOW has relied extensively on direct-mail campaigns for fund raising and in 1977 profited more than $150,000 through ERA Walkathons held in many cities. Some funds are sent directly to the states; others are spent by the national office for financing strategy conferences, printed materials, staff salaries, and seeding state fund-raising efforts.

Although unable to commit economic resources at the level of BPW, LWV, or NOW, other national associations have also been effective in coordinating and supporting state ratification activities, by means ranging from provision of small grants to publication of brochures for general distribution.

Taken as a whole, these ventures by national groups supporting the ERA appear to be best characterized by the interest group conflict model. Although, as specified by the community conflict model, groups and individuals from outside the individual states have been actively involved in ERA ratification, the situation is not quite analogous to that of community conflicts over civil rights or fluoridation. Here the "outsiders" are merely the national staff members of organizations providing certain services to their long-established state chapters.

While the amendment was before Congress, many national staff members had become quite knowledgeable on the subject. Research materials and other data disseminated by them to state chapters should have been especially prized by state legislators.

In terms of purely organizational efficiency, such assistance to the state chapters is invaluable. Since all states were reviewing the amendment at approximately the same time, it is more expedient to centralize the national group's research and publications undertakings, rather than assigning to each state the task of developing its own literature. Given the importance of adequate financing to group success, centralized fund-raising efforts are also an asset. The national headquarters, with its nationwide constituency, can continue to appeal to *all* members, including those in the states where the ERA has already been ratified.

Finally, the example of national coalitions has facilitated the formation of group alliances on the state level. Despite the frequent lack of continuity between the various national coordinating committees, coalitions, and task forces, each has been better organized, more active, and more cohesive than its predecessor.

Activity on the National Level against the ERA

The patterns of activity of national organizations actively opposing the Equal Rights Amendment have been quite different from those of supporters. Discussion of opposition groups must deal less with interorganizational coordination than with the phenomenon of ad hoc organizations, overlapping memberships, and spin-off groups. (See Appendix E for a list of associations opposed to the ERA.)

The active participation of the John Birch Society itself in the ERA controversy is unusual in that the major resistance to the amendment has been led by ad hoc groups. Yet its role in discouraging ERA ratification is reflective of the long recognized linkages among conservative groups. The Society first officially took note of the ERA in November 1972, several months after congressional passage.[2] Only when passage seemed near, did its founder and director Robert Welch become alarmed and urge the membership to "plunge in and help to relegate this subversive proposal to early and complete oblivion."[3]

Society members in Utah had been working since December 1972 against the ERA, through their ad hoc association called HOTDOG (Humanitarians Opposed to Degrading Our Girls). In the *John Birch Society Bulletin* of May 1973, a Wisconsin ad hoc group POW (Protect Our Women) with Birch beginnings was saluted for its role in defeating a state ERA referendum. Birch members are also leaders in other organizations active against the amendment. On the National Council of the John Birch Society in 1974, for example, were Thomas J. Anderson, chairperson and 1976 Presidential candidate of the American Party, and Clarence Manion of the Manion Forum Trust Fund, believed to be a major source of funding for the ERA opposition movement. The alleged Society affiliation of Phyllis Schlafly has long been a subject of considerable speculation. The March 1960 *Bulletin* praised her as a "very loyal member of the John Birch Society." The general feeling of those following Schlafly's career is that although she may have once been a member, she has since resigned in order to broaden her political base.

Important though the John Birch Society and its members have been, Stop ERA is by far the most prominent group opposing ERA ratification. When a proponent charges that the opposition shows signs of being engineered single-handedly by a leader on the national level, there is no doubt that the leader in question is Stop ERA's founder and chairperson, Phyllis Schlafly, of Alton, Illinois. Author or coauthor of several books (including the Barry Goldwater campaign classic *A Choice Not An Echo*), two-time unsuccessful congressional candidate, past vice-president of the National Federation of Republican Women's Clubs (NFRWC), and editor and publisher of the *Phyllis Schlafly Report*, an ultra-conservative political newsletter begun in 1968 after her defeat for the NFRWC presidency, Ms. Schlafly has given unity to her convictions in many states through the provision of literature and educational materials, legislative testimony, and personal visits to the states at crucial times during the decision process.

Her February 1972 *Report* was devoted entirely to "What's Wrong with 'Equal Rights' for Women" and was her first public comment on the amendment. Not until late 1972 did she establish the National Committee to Stop ERA. By mid-January 1973, the association had several thousand members and was active in 26 states, being strongest in the South and Mid-West. She had also formed a blue-ribbon National Committee of Endorsers Against ERA, which included the wives of seven members of Congress. During 1972, her monthly *Report* dealt with the ERA only occasionally. Beginning in 1973, a special supplement on the subject was included in almost every issue and was widely disseminated and made use of by all opponents, regardless of group affiliation.

Like the John Birch Society, Stop ERA has given birth to a number of separate ad hoc groups, some operating nation-wide and some solely in one state. AWARE (American Women Already Richly Endowed) was founded by Ms. Schlafly as an instrument for writing letters opposing the amendment to legislators in unratified states. Evelyn Pitsche, legal advisor to Stop ERA, formed Scratch Women's Lib at the request of disgruntled members of groups committed to the ERA. Various state units of Stop ERA adopted names pointedly descriptive of their objections to the amendment, such as the League for the Protection of Women and Children.

The only other individual to attract attention as a national figure in the ERA opposition is Jaquie Davison, wife of a San Diego chiropractor and founder of Happiness of Womanhood.

HOW was set up in July 1971 after Ms. Davison first became aware of the proposed amendment, then before Congress. By December 1972, HOW and a spin-off organization, the League of Housewives, claimed 10,000 members in all 50 states. Like Ms. Schlafly, Ms. Davison has appeared as a witness at legislative ERA hearings. She has published her autobiography, *I Am a Housewife*, and issues a monthly *Newsletter* for her membership. Some anti-ERA literature has also been produced by HOW for general distribution.

The community conflict model accurately describes the formation of these new partisan organizations such as HOW, Stop ERA, and even the John Birch Society's ad hoc groups, formed solely to contest the Equal Rights Amendment. They and their leaders have played major roles in initiating and expanding disharmony concerning the subject throughout the country. But whereas national organizations supporting the amendment have acted at the request of their state chapters, ad hoc groups such as Stop ERA and HOW have had to first *organize* state chapters in order to mobilize state residents.

The interest group conflict model also applies to certain of the organizational characteristics of these opposition groups. But in respect to their activities being associated with non-ratification, this model offers little assistance. No apparent effort has gone into establishing formal alliances with other like-minded groups at the national level, although those persons holding leadership positions in several anti-ERA associations may be serving as linchpins. Nor, as new organizations, are the ad hoc groups likely to approximate the profile of the effective interest group in terms of a large and geographically broad membership, a well-developed internal organization, and an established reputation in the political system.

Given the importance of group services to legislators, particularly the provision of research, national opposition forces would again appear at a disadvantage. Compared with the production of pro-ERA literature by national organizations, relatively little anti-ERA literature has been generated by the national opposing forces. Aside from the widely circulated

Phyllis Schlafly Report and the mimeographed literature from HOW, there have appeared only a brochure of excerpts from the minority views of Senator Sam Ervin; reprints of the *American Opinion* article by John Schmitz; and a few articles in other politically conservative newspapers and magazines which have taken an anti-ERA editorial stand. Frequently, these "articles" were reprinted verbatim from Ms. Schlafly's *Report*.

While there is no gauge for comparing the adequacy of either side's financing, the contrast between their relative openness concerning their sources of funding is great. Whereas proponent organizations have conducted public drives for contributions and have reported periodically on their success, the opposition's statements on this subject have raised more questions than they have answered. John F. McManus, director of public relations for the John Birch Society, has denied that the national Society has financially supported anti-ERA groups or that it maintains any special ERA fund.[4] Ms. Davison has maintained that her husband is paying her bills, as are the husbands of other women in HOW. Ms. Schlafly has repeatedly refused to admit either to receiving any money from the John Birch Society or any other conservative group or to using her own Eagle Trust Fund, established after her defeat for the NFRWC presidency as a conduit for contributions from her supporters, to finance Stop ERA. She claims her activities are underwritten by her husband and through other contributions, none of which has exceeded $100. "Local people pay my plane fare when they want me to speak. They distribute my newsletter and buy extras for eight dollars a hundred to send out."[5]

Yet much skepticism has been expressed concerning her explanation of the financing of Stop ERA. The scope of opposition efforts in the states involves sizable expenditures; the late Ann Scott as NOW legislative vice-president estimated that a minimum of $30,000 went into anti-ERA lobbying efforts in each unratified state in 1973.[6] Speculation about monetary sources has focused upon the conservative foundations whose newsletters so frequently contain Ms. Schlafly's essays; the John Birch Society, with its reported $8 million annual budget; and several major insurance companies.[7] In the wake of revelations about the financing of Richard Nixon's 1972 campaign, this reticence to divulge their sources of funding should be considered a debt.

Another area in which the opposition has been disadvantaged is their public reputations or perceived legitimacy. The actively opposed national groups are primarily those espousing ultraright political views. Two exceptions are the AFL-CIO, which opposed the amendment until October 1973, and the National Council of Catholic Women, which continues to be hostile. Even so, opposition has not been systematic throughout the Church or the labor movement.

Internally divided over the ERA, the AFL-CIO, in 1972 and 1973, had become increasingly uncomfortable in its alliance with its ideological enemies of the far right. Labor leaders began to fear that in the flush of victory over defeating the ERA, these extreme conservatives, having newly politicized many citizens, would use their increased strength against labor's legislative programs. With the unanimous endorsement of the amendment in 1973 by the AFL-CIO in convention and the formation in 1974 of the Coalition of Labor Union Women (CLUW) to work for, among other goals, ERA ratification, the claims of the opposition to speak for the working-class woman were thoroughly negated.

Like organized labor before 1973, Catholic groups, too, are split over the ERA. Nuns' organizations have been actively in support, with several nuns taking prominent leadership positions in state ERA coalitions. The Church hierarchy has said little on the matter, although some bishops have spoken out against it locally. Catholic laywomen have worked for the ERA and have attempted to portray the NCCW's opposition as unrepresentative. They claim that the Council's initial vote to oppose the ERA was taken 10 years ago when consciousness or concern about equality for women was minimal. In early 1974, a national ad hoc group, Catholic Women for the ERA, was formed.

On balance, then, proponents, secure in their own broad-based coalition of well-established mainstream organizations, have felt free to call attention to the radical right composition of the opposition forces. In defense, the opposition has charged supporters of the amendment with using the

"McCarthy" tactic of "guilt by association" in linking ad hoc anti-ERA groups with the discredited John Birch Society, the Ku Klux Klan, and the National States' Rights Party.

State Organization and the ERA: The Proponent Groups

After congressional passage, the fate of the ERA rested ultimately with the state legislatures, as has been noted. Given the nature of the support offered state chapters by their national headquarters, the interest groups favoring the amendment theoretically should have been more effective than those in opposition. They should have had advantages regarding both tactical and economic resources. Considering the national groups on both sides of the issue, it was expected that the proponent groups would occupy a more respected place in the community, be better-known, and be accorded greater legitimacy by decision makers. Further, proponents should have formed well-developed group alliances on the state level.

In general, the experience in the states in organizing pro-ERA coalitions paralleled that on the national level. At the close of the 1973 legislative sessions, very few active state ERA coalitions existed; some were just beginning to get organized. By mid-1974, 14 of the 17 unratified states had developed extensive, statewide pro-ERA coalitions, several of which had even established a central headquarters, with full-time salaried office staff and WATS lines, in a major urban business district or in the capitol area. Some coalitions consisted of fewer than 20 member-organizations; others claimed more than 100.

Although the groups particularly active in support of ERA varied somewhat from state to state, the following organizations were more often involved: BPW, LWV, AAUW, Common Cause, NOW, NWPC, and the General Federation of Women's Clubs (GFWC). These not only provided the bulk of the volunteers requisite for the ERA campaign itself, but also were instrumental in raising the necessary funds. In addition to relying on individual and organizational donations, the coalitions or individual member-groups sponsored a variety of imaginative fund-raising activities. A series of Louisiana Red Beans and Rice Dinners, sponsored by local chapters of NOW, secured several hundred dollars. Florida's Men for ERA, in cooperation with the Florida pro-ERA coalition, sponsored a tennis match between politicians and women tennis players from local colleges. Elsewhere, the ERA fund was augmented through button and bumper sticker sales, garage sales, flea markets, and receptions for prominent women such as Gloria Steinem.

The gains anticipated from the formation of coalitions are of two kinds: an increase in available resources and an increase in the number of tactical options. A coalition's basic purpose is coordination, insuring that member-organizations are in fact accomplishing what they are best able to do in achieving a desired result—in this case, ratification of the ERA. Thus, it is a strength of a coalition that member groups have different strategies and tactics, but this can also produce internal conflicts. Some groups are more "activist" than others. The orientation and behavior of a "women's rights" group such as NOW will vary from that of the LWV or AAUW. The patterns of cooperation between proponent groups in the three states studied all exhibited this diversity and, in one case, the internal dissension of broad political coalitions.

Texas   No formal coalition of pro-ERA groups existed in Texas in 1972. Because the special three-day legislative session at which the amendment was ratified was called with little advance notice by the Governor and convened only six days after congressional passage, there was no time nor, as was shown by the near-unanimous ratification, any need to form such an alliance. Many of the group leaders interviewed had to be reminded of the exact date and circumstances of Texas ratification. Some spoke at length of their activities on behalf of ERA, only to realize, upon closer questioning, that it was the state Equal Legal Rights Amendment (ELRA) for which they had worked.[8] The AFL–CIO in Texas, which ordinarily supports women's rights, remained neutral in 1972, in deference to the national organization's stance. The Business and Professional Women's Clubs, leader of a coalition of women's groups working for passage of the state ELRA, was involved during the 1972 Special Session, as were NOW and the Texas Women's Political Caucus. Other groups, which must be considered potential members of a coalition for ERA had such been necessary, had worked together for ELRA passage and again during the short-lived move in 1973 to "reconsider" Texas ratification. These included, in addition to those already mentioned: the Texas Federation of Women's Clubs, the League of Women Voters, Common Cause, the Women's Equity Action League, AAUW, the Communication Workers of America, Home Demonstration Clubs, and various church groups. Not until 1975, with the appearance of an organized movement to rescind, was a statewide coalition (Texans for the ERA) formed.

Illinois   As in Texas, there was no formal coalition of pro-ERA groups in Illinois during the 1972 legislative session, although individual groups lobbied for the ERA in the state capitol in Springfield. Since that time several coalitions have been formed. The first, called ERA Central, came into being after the resolution first failed in 1972. It was organized by five organizations—BPW, LWV, NOW, AAUW, and Federally Employed Women (FEW)—which remained its prime movers. By 1974, ERA Central was officially composed of 103 member-organizations, including a broad range of religious, ethnic, and racial groups; several radical feminist groups such as the Chicago Women's Liberation Union; and a group called the American Divorce Association for Men.

After the amendment's legislative defeat in 1974, the lobbyists for LWV and NOW took the lead in setting up the Illnois Ratification Council to coordinate member-group activities and to involve these outside Chicago more actively than did ERA Central. Care was taken, however, to present the Council as an organization complementary to ERA Central.

In the spring of 1976, all organizations and coalitions supporting the amendment in Illinois merged to form ERA Illnois, organized along the lines of ERAmerica. An experienced full-time campaign director was engaged to head a paid office staff. And two prominent Illinois citizens, representing the two major political parties, were asked to serve as cochairs.

As the longest-lived (nearly four years) Illinois coalition, ERA Central provides the best example of the level of formal organization attained by ERA supporters. It was highly systematized, having a full-time executive director, a part-time office manager, and a number of state chairpersons who were responsible for activities such as financing, public relations, labor relations, and lobbying. Weekly strategy meetings were held at its headquarters in the part of the Chicago central business district known as "the Loop." Several regular newsletters supplemented the WATS line linking the legislative districts with the headquarters.

ERA Central, from all appearances, had adequate financing. Voluntary contributions and Speaker's Bureau fees helped keep the coalition solvent. Among other fund-raising projects, Illinois groups were able to obtain the cooperation of local artists for an auction; the Second City satirical group for a benefit; and even a rebate from a local grocery chain. The Chicago Junior Chamber of Commerce did much of the printing for ERA Central.

Although ERA Central was located in, and undoubtedly drew its greatest support from, the Chicago area, it attempted to be a statewide coalition. Each legislative district had a coordinator who was personally responsible for contacting legislators in that area. Beginning with the 1974 legislative session, a full-time paid lobbyist was sent to Springfield. There was general recognition, however, that ERA Central was largely a "paper" coalition, in that member-groups as a whole were not actively brought into the activities, only certain of their members. While some participants reported internal division over tactics and some problems stemming from the assimilation of new leaders into an ongoing group, ERA Central by and large presented a public face of cohesiveness.

Perhaps organized labor, a genuine force in Illinois politics, was the deepest disappointment inside ERA Central. As one activist explained:

> Labor is definitely a sore point ... is not really as active as it could be. Labor is accustomed to people coming to it and ERA

Central doesn't have the staff to do this. The AFL–CIO head is privately opposed to ERA and won't work for or against it. A couple of labor votes did switch with the AFL–CIO endorsement but we were told in December (1973) that COPE would include ERA as an issue for support, which they did not do.

Another potential source of internal divisiveness within pro-ERA coalitions is the role of radical feminists and lesbian groups. The Illinois ratification movement has apparently not found this to be a problem, either because of the political sophistication or the disinterest of such groups there. One proponent favored the former explanation; a second leader saw it differently:

> Gays are only a slight problem. It's bad enough having NOW as a coalition member. An Illinois Small Business Association figure sent out an anti-NOW letter. Ms. Schlafly also singles out NOW for its radicalism and lesbianism. But no radicals are demanding to be included. They're cool; they understand.

> Eighteen- to twenty-five-year-olds should be flocking to the ERA Central office but they're not because the women working with Third World groups think we're just copping out with this approach. Radical women are not really interested in ERA because they feel Third World people need *more* rights. There are lesbians in ERA Central but others choose to ignore that fact.

Georgia   Internal cohesion has been extremely problematic for the groups in Georgia supporting the amendment. As a result, two separate coalitions working for ratification coexist in that state: the Georgia (Statewide) Coalition for the ERA, composed of approximately 15 organizations, including LWV, BPW, AAUW, Church Women United, Communication Workers of America, and the Georgia Federation of Women's Clubs; and Georgians for the ERA (G-ERA), designed as a grass-roots mass movement for unaffiliated women in the state and led primarily by members of the Socialist Workers Party (SWP) and the Atlanta Lesbian Feminist Alliance (ALFA). The new feminist groups NOW and the Georgia Women's Political Caucus (GWPC) were caught in the middle and chose to cooperate with G-ERA in some of its projects.

Preceding the formation of these dual coalitions, however, attempts to coordinate the activities of the pro-ERA groups in Georgia followed the pattern previously noted nationally and in Illinois. In early January, 1973, concurrent with the convening of the first legislature that could consider the ERA, a loose coalition of all pro-ERA groups was formed. There was, according to one Statewide leader, "no structure, little direction, and tremendous jealousy among groups to assert themselves as working uniquely for ERA." During the 45-day legislative session, the activist groups were described as "very cooperative" by leaders of the Statewide Coalition. Still, as one new feminist leader put it: "The activist groups felt a need to curb themselves in order to remain in the coalition and conservative groups felt themselves being pushed by activist groups."

In the spring of 1973, following the legislative session, a meeting was called to form another coalition with a more formal structure. But now the diverse political orientations of the groups came to the surface. NOW, ALFA, and the SWP vetoed a structured coalition. They preferred only a loose arrangement for sharing information, not formal meetings at which motions were made and votes taken on tactics and strategies. Given this disunity, the meeting was adjourned and no coalition was established.

G-ERA had been created in May, 1973. And in July 1973, the Statewide Coalition, including at that time the GWPC and NOW, was organized. Aside from Statewide's cooperation with G-ERA in sponsoring Congresswoman Martha Griffiths' Georgia appearance, each coalition pursued its own strategy.

G-ERA leaders felt they should be allowed to work openly for the ERA. ("Judge us on the basis of the job we've done, organizing, and push your prejudices against socialists and lesbians aside.") They also felt strongly that the strategies and tactics associated with social movements ("the politics of disorder") should be viewed as legitimate by all of ERA's supporters. For their part, the Statewide Coalition could not accept the participation of lesbians ("ALFA just scares people") nor, in the end, the participation of NOW and the GWPC. Although one member of Statewide professed to be sympathetic with NOW and the Caucus ("They need the publicity and their day in the sun"), she felt "they aren't doing ERA any good."

Despite their opposition to structure in a coalition, G-ERA appeared to have a bureaucratic form of organization. A headquarters near the capitol was staffed by full-time salaried workers. Weekly meetings were held and a newsletter published at short intervals. From the newsletter, it appeared that G-ERA had been successful in drawing support from all the larger cities in the state. Relying primarily upon individual contributions, sale items, and various fund-raising events, G-ERA had adequate financing despite inaccessibility to major national ERA funds or a large preexisting state membership.

The Statewide Coalition (described tongue-in-cheek by one member as "the group of middle-aged women who did not understand democracy") held meetings once a week, usually in a member's home. Each member-organization sent one representative; after discussion, majority votes determined the coalition's policies. No central headquarters or permanent staff was maintained. No special fund raising was attempted, although each member-group shared its resources (e.g., the League's WATS line) with other coalition members. Between meetings, group leaders communicated by telephone; no newsletter was published. The Coalition maintained such a low organizational profile that the national LWV's first *ERA Yes* newsletter (December 1973) listed G-ERA as the "official" Georgia coalition contact, omitting the Statewide Coalition, headed by one of its own members!

The split in pro-ERA ranks became public on January 11, 1974, shortly after the convening of the Georgia legislature. The Atlanta *Journal* revealed that Gloria Steinem, at the request of the Statewide Coalition, had canceled her appearance at a parade organized by G-ERA. A Statewide spokesperson estimated that, at worst, the public bickering cost the amendment five to ten votes in the legislature later that month. The schism, however, has endured.

State Organizations and the ERA: The Opponent Groups

In contrast to the numerous newspaper stories concerning the activities of pro-ERA groups and coalitions, accounts of comparable opposition activities are few. Opponents received press coverage, to be sure, but opposition in the states was presented as less of an organized group activity than as a series of actions by individuals, either with or without a formal group affiliation.

When a group was linked with opposition to the ERA, only rarely was that group an established organization such as the Daughters of the American Revolution, the National Council of Catholic Women, or even the John Birch Society. Ad hoc groups formed around the ERA seemed to have multiplied at the state level. And, like the national organizations in opposition to the amendment, the state groups have also been very defensive about their financial sources. For example, an ERA adversary in North Carolina, a member of the John Birch Society, denied receiving funds from that group and gave a sworn testimony to that effect to a senate committee. As a result, attempts to address questions as to formal organization, group alliances, and adequacy of financing were inevitably less successful here than with proponent groups. Such matters were often irrelevant to the opposition's methods of operations.

Texas   None of the members of the Texas legislature or leaders of the proponent groups were aware of any organized opposition to the ERA at the time of ratification. As one opposition leader in Texas explained:

> Although the National Council of Catholic Women, John Birch Society, and the Daughters of the American Revolution are in opposition on the national level, local Texas members didn't get anything going. They only had three days to stop ratification. It's hard to do anything effective in that short a time.

Opposition groups thus were forced to fight a rearguard action by seeking rescission.[9] Aside from an abortive movement in 1973 to rescind, led by elements of the John Birch Society in Texas, there was little overt opposition activity until 1974. That year two ad hoc groups emerged: the Committee to Restore Women's Rights (CRWR) and Women Who Want to Be Women (WWWW). Support for these two groups has come primarily from the memberships of other organizations, including the John Birch Society, the American Party, HOW, Pro-America, NCCW, DAR, Women for Constitutional

Government, Stop ERA, and local PTA and fundamentalist church groups. CRWR and WWWW members do not ordinarily mention their association with these other groups except in response to a direct question.

No systematic assessment of the structural development of these two ad hoc organizations and the adequacy of their financing was attempted since this study concerned itself primarily with the period of ERA ratification in Texas. However, both WWWW and CRWR have attempted to build statewide organizations by forming local chapters; CRWR, for example, was said to have over 40 chapters. During the final weeks of the 1975 legislative session, a joint office near the capitol was shared by the two groups. As for financing, WWWW has publicly revealed that at least some of its support comes from the Parker Chiropractic Research Foundation, established by Dr. James Parker, a close friend of HOW leader Jaquie Davison. And the Mary Kay Cosmetics firm, until threatened by a national boycott to be publicized in *Ms.* magazine, openly distributed WWWW literature. But according to a CRWR spokesperson:

> We're financed strictly by individual donations. There's no tax money, no foundation grants for us. I'm amazed to read of "well-financed" opposition to ERA. I know of none; everywhere it's a matter of scrouging for every penny. I give up a beauty shop appointment occasionally to pay the printing costs of literature . . . two-dollar, five-dollar, ten-dollar donations, that's all.

Illinois   Organized opposition to the ERA was evident in Illinois from the first days of legislative consideration there, as would be expected in the home state of Phyllis Schlafly. But although most of the national opposition groups active in Illinois work in close cooperation with Stop ERA, they have also maintained their separate identities. For example, the NCCW and the John Birch Society have circulated their own literature and provided spokespersons at legislative hearings and other public forums. Pro-America and HOW have also been independently prominent adversaries.

As in other states, ad hoc groups have appeared in Illinois. One, called Right to Be a Woman,[10] has attracted many dissenting members of proponent groups and of the NCCW. A second is the International Anti-"Women's Liberation"

League (AWLL), an organization believing "men should be men and women should be women" and which has taken the diaper pin as its symbol.

In general, opposition groups have not emphasized formal organizational structure. Even Stop ERA, although technically having a complete network of legislative district chairpersons, has concentrated on only a few areas in the state for real grass-roots organization. Group leaders work in close direct cooperation with each other, chiefly by telephone. Many opposition women were quite candid concerning this:

> I know the other women who are opposed to the ERA. We talk on the phone and mail things back and forth if someone hears something or of a new article. We've done more to educate ourselves on the Amendment than to try to do anything about it because I don't think many people are doing anything.

> It's a different kind of movement. It's more of an individual thing.

As has been the pattern nationally and in other states, no opponent interviewed in Illinois reported receiving financial support from a national group. Each maintained that everyone in her group was "doing it out of her own pocket":

> I haven't tried to get outside funding. I feel it's worth my personal time and money. It hasn't cost a lot really. I'm on ERA Central's mailing list and they have lots of fund raisers and appeals for money. But I've never been asked for money by [ERA] opponents.

Georgia Opposition to the ERA has been organized in Georgia since the early days of the 1973 legislative session. Although, again, there is no official coalition of groups in opposition, Stop ERA in practice serves in that capacity here. Several organizations are represented within Stop ERA, including HOW, DAR, the John Birch Society, the American Party, and dissenting members of the Atlanta Women's Club (part of the Georgia Federation of Women's Clubs). Interestingly, there has been no real involvement of fundamentalist religious groups here, unlike Texas. The telephone is relied upon for communication; opposition members also encounter each other at legislative hearings or at an occasional strategy meeting. Stop ERA is reported to exercise influence in all counties of the state. Availing herself of personal contacts and a mailing list compiled at the first legislative hearing in 1973, the state chairperson of Stop ERA has traveled statewide organizing chapters and training her membership.

Like opponents in Texas and Illinois, the opposition groups in Georgia appear to be cohesive, with only two exceptions. There is still some hesitancy to openly admit an association with the John Birch Society. Society members are aware that Birchers are unpopular and thus they have deliberately not distributed the *American Opinion* reprint in Georgia. Opponents also complain about their association in the media with the National States' Rights Party and its chairperson, J. B. Stoner, noted racist, anti-Semite, and perennial candidate for state office. Stoner cheerfully acknowledges that his views on race and religion make him publicly unacceptable to other groups and so he has worked against the ERA on his own.

Georgia opposition groups also reported that their activities were financed by personal donations, and that no funds were provided by any individual or organization outside the state. However, in light of Ms. Schlafly's explanations concerning local financing of her own travels, it is interesting to note the circumstances surrounding her first appearance in Georgia and the establishment of Stop ERA there. According to a member of that organization:

> A group of conservative anti-ERA people, very loosely organized, were responsible for bringing Mrs. Schlafly down. Some voluntary contributions were collected for Mrs. Schlafly's expenses. I'm not sure she ever got all of it. I was not in on the groundwork of formation of Stop ERA, but we quickly organized a group when Phyllis was coming down to appear before the House.

One opposition leader put it more bluntly: "Schlafly has her own money."

Some Personal and Political Characteristics of ERA Activists

Both the interest group and community conflict models place considerable importance on certain personal characteristics of participants in political conflicts. Each presents a different profile of the typical activist, however. The interest group conflict model suggests that participants in the ERA conflict will be predominantly of a higher social status than the average American woman and members of a group regularly engaging in political disputes. Relative success here stems from perceived "legitimacy" based in part on past political experience and a higher social status. The community conflict model discounts the significance of social status; in certain cases, recruits from the *lowest* stratum may be the most valuable. Nor is past political experience necessarily associated with persuasiveness, given the emergence of ad hoc groups attracting members of the community who ordinarily do not participate in group politics.

A growing body of research has accumulated on the social backgrounds and personality structures of the new feminists and antifeminists.[11] The groups which have become involved with the ERA, however, do not neatly fall into these two categories. The new feminist groups such as NOW and the NWPC are only one part of the broad-based coalition supporting the ERA. And although many of the politically conservative groups in opposition are antifeminist in philosophy, they are basically multigoal organizations. Thus, interviews with the leaders of groups active in ERA ratification were of special importance in discovering some of the personal characteristics of those participating in this conflict.[12]

Personal Backgrounds

As a group, the opposition leaders represented a broader socioeconomic background but a narrower occupational background than did their proponent counterparts. (See table 3.1.) In Illinois, the high social status among opposition leaders was derived largely from husbands in the professions and business. But in both Illinois and Georgia, a few opposition leaders were employed as college deans, public school teachers, or independent businesswomen (a real estate agent and a manufacturing company owner). Some lower middle-class housewives emerged as opposition leaders, as well. Although several opposition spokespersons stated that their membership was drawn from a variety of educational and

TABLE 3.1
Occupational Backgrounds of Group Leaders

Occupation	Proponents		Opponents	
	Male	*Female*	*Male*	*Female*
Business	2	5	1	2
Education	0	4	0	2
Law	1	4	1	0
Labor union official	2	1	0	0
Housewife	0	10	0	9
Other	0	3	2	0
TOTAL	5	27	4	13

SOURCE: Personal interviews with group leaders.

occupational backgrounds, all viewed their natural constituency as the middle-income and lower middle-income
housewife.

Proponent leaders in Illinois were, with few exceptions,
employed full-time outside the home. Their counterparts in
Georgia and Texas varied according to group affiliation.
Leaders of traditional women's groups (with the exception of
BPW) were most commonly upper middle-class housewives.
Leaders of the newer groups, without exception, had outside
jobs. Although the types of positions held by these women
varied, there were several public employees (primarily
lawyers) and others working in some sector of communications (public relations, advertising, consulting) or education. Most would be considered as holding managerial-
professional positions. Again, the types of members described
by proponent leaders covered a wide range. Proponents have
tried, with some success, to mobilize college students in
Georgia, and a few black women actively participated in both
Illinois and Georgia.

Political Backgrounds

The political prominence and past experience of those who
became involved with ERA varied greatly, even within the
same group. Some legislators were acquainted with those

who contacted them concerning the ERA. In particular, those who were their constituents and/or who agreed with the legislator on the issue were more likely to be known personally. On the other hand, many legislators could not recall any prior contacts with ERA activists. Both sides included some politically experienced leaders. The ERA had also proven a powerful activator for many women who had not previously been politically involved. In general, proponent group leaders more often reported memberships which had been involved previously in working for or against a bill before the state legislature. Groups such as the League, BPW, and AAUW, after all, have long been engaged in legislative lobbying.

Texas　In Texas, even the leaders of the new feminist groups, NOW and the NWPC, had had previous legislative experience (as a paid lobbyist and as a legislative aide). Other groups which had worked to put the state ELRA on the ballot numbered many politically experienced members. In contrast, the leaders of the two ad hoc opposition groups in Texas were recent residents of the state, although one had had previous campaign and lobbying experience as the niece of a state legislator.

Georgia　The situation was much the same in Georgia. The legislative chairperson of BPW had been active on behalf of women's rights in the legislature for over 30 years and was a well-known figure in the capitol. Other Statewide Coalition groups had members extensively acquainted with lobbying. One had also managed two successful congressional campaigns. Although the membership of the new feminist groups were often political neophytes, they had experienced leaders and were quick to learn the nuances of legislative politics. Said one leader:

> Previous to ERA, we'd had no involvement in legislative lobbying. ERA has really brought women into the legislative process. We've learned how to get a bill drafted and an attorney who will do it. We've found contacts and advisors.

Even the leaders of G-ERA, a group formed to mobilize unaffiliated women, were themselves veterans of the civil rights and abortion reform movements.

With the exception of the John Birch Society members, most of the people opposing the ERA in Georgia had had little or no political experience. According to a (male) opposition leader:

> The ERA has gotten more people involved and interested than any issue I've ever seen. Women aroused can accomplish a lot . . . Because of their concern for the home, they became desperate.

The Georgia chairperson of HOW had no prior experience. And although the state chairperson of Stop ERA reported that she had personally been politically active, many of her members had never been to the capitol or written a letter to a public official before becoming involved on this issue.

Illinois   Due, no doubt, to the political prominence of Ms. Schlafly, more politically experienced women have been drawn into leadership positions in the Illinois opposition, a fact which is not lost on the proponents. As one lamented:

> ——— is a "good works" volunteer. Schlafly is prominent nationally. ——— is prominent in the Chicago area through the Republican Party. ——— is prominent in terms of BPW and Democratic politics. They're not neophytes . . . Who do we have on our side? Nobody! Oh, we've all been active in our communities. . . .

However, only two Illinois opposition group leaders reported that their political and community activities had included legislative lobbying. Although two leaders said that other members of their groups had worked on legislation in the past, most opposition groups were described as being composed of political amateurs.

Unlike Texas and Georgia, where the state leaders of major (pro-ERA) women's organizations personally assumed leadership roles in the ERA conflict, in Illinois a subleadership class within such groups emerged as ERA specialists. Inevitably, these women were somewhat less experienced than those in the top leadership ranks. Furthermore, in attempting to build a statewide structure, ERA Central had to rely on many relatively inexperienced persons. To quote one ERA Central state coordinator:

> The people in the districts don't have that much political pull. They're ordinary constituents who legislators are supposed to listen to. They don't.

Although one group leader expressed some concern about the "well-intentioned but politically unsophisticated amateurs" who have become involved in behalf of the ERA, proponent groups such as the League, AAUW, and NOW in Illinois mentioned numerous politically experienced members. Of the three full-time lobbyists for ERA in Springfield in 1974, only one had hitherto been unfamiliar with lobbying. One had served as legislative aide, and the other had a background in Republican party politics which equaled that of Ms. Schlafly.

"Fear and Loathing" and the ERA

Although no question was asked explicitly concerning each side's image of the other, several such comments were spontaneously volunteered. These are significant, given the observation that as community conflicts expand, resort to personal slander becomes increasingly prevalent.

Perhaps because of the feeling of "sisterhood" engendered by the new feminist movement, acrimonious attacks upon the opposition by proponent women were rare. The latter seemed confident in their own superior knowledge and training and were concerned about their "misguided but sincere" opponents. Representative comments were:

> They're so naive. I'm afraid of what is going to happen to them. They can't debate. If it doesn't come out of the *Schlafly Report*, they can't articulate it.

> The people seemed programmed like they had been told: "This is the wrong thing, here's the money, go out and do something about it."

Interestingly, the most derogatory description of the opposition came from a male proponent, who termed them "a motley sleazy right-wing bunch of zealots."

Members of the opposition were not nearly so charitable in their assessments of proponents. While deploring the polarization that ERA has created among women, one member of

HOW expressed her belief that all proponents were atheists. Additional pejoratives included: "rude," "profane," "young jeans-wearing loud radicals," "nihilistic versions of T. S. Eliot's 'Hollow Men,'" and "women but not ladies." Here, then, the community conflict model seems to better characterize the behavior of opponents than that of proponents.

Community, State, and National Elites and the ERA

Another potentially important group of participants in ERA ratification is the community and governmental leadership. Elite support is important because prominent names make news. Furthermore, these leaders help form public opinion. Members of both the public at large and the legislature can be influenced by their value judgments. Support from other elected and appointed government officials is especially important in influencing legislators. For example, a strong relationship has been observed between gubernatorial support and interest group success.[13] And the effectiveness of the group member who is also a legislator has often been noted.

While acknowledging the importance of elite support, particularly to those seeking adoption of a new policy, the community conflict model indicates that such support often will not be available to either side. As conflict increases, these established leaders often withdraw from active participation in the dispute.

Only proponent groups have made any major attempt to involve community and state leaders, the political parties, or sympathetic members of the state and national bureaucracy in the debate over ratification. The opposition has instead criticized federal and state governmental involvement, carried on, they complain, at taxpayers' expense.

Although former Congresswoman and ERA sponsor Martha Griffiths has made some personal appearances in unratified states, the activities of Presidents Gerald Ford and Jimmy Carter and their families, White House staff members, and the U.S. Citizens' Advisory Council on the Status of Women have been most prominent and thus most subject to attack by opposition forces. In 1977, President and Mrs. Carter phoned state legislators on behalf of the ERA shortly before crucial floor votes. Earlier, Betty Ford and Nixon staff members Anne Armstrong and Jill Ruckelshaus actively supported the amendment.

The staff and members of the Citizens' Advisory Council have testified for the ERA at legislative hearings and have appeared at other public forums. Both the Council and the Women's Bureau of the Labor Department see their activities as public education on the pros and cons of the ERA. They also point out that their ERA literature represents only a small portion of their total publications program.

The opposition nonetheless has charged that this support proves that the ERA is a federal power-grab. They have also claimed that the federal government is secretly funding ERA lobbyists at the state capitols through the Department of Labor's "Emergency Unemployment" grants, funneled through the state commissions on the status of women.

It is true that many state commissions on the status of women (CSW) have been very energetic in support of the ERA. Most governors in unratified states have formally endorsed the amendment and some governors (and their wives) have actively supported it with personal lobbying. Assistance from political parties in the states, however, has been limited, despite the ERA's inclusion in both national platforms in 1972.

The opposition has not been entirely without elite support, having received aid from certain political party groups, most notably some Republican women's clubs aligned with the Goldwater-Schlafly wing. Governors in Arizona, Virginia, and Mississippi have variously taken positions of outright opposition or of neutrality. Opponents in North Carolina were unexpectedly abetted when legislators' wives invited Ms. Schlafly to testify at hearings on the ERA.

Perhaps the most effective ERA opponents within the government have been female legislators. Although the vast majority of the latter support the amendment and serve as chief sponsors in many states, the fact that any division among women legislators exists has seemed to operate to the advantage of the opposition.

Texas   In Texas, the formal legislative leadership—the house speaker and the lieutenant governor—supported the ERA. Governor Preston Smith, at the request of one proponent, urged the assembled joint houses to consider and ratify the amendment during the March 1972 special session.[14] The only two female legislators also were in support. And members of the state CSW were requested to contact their legislators on behalf of the ERA.

In the later rescission movement, opponents received no support from state officials, community leaders, party groups, or female legislators. Governor Dolph Briscoe, however, refused to publicly reveal his position on the ERA as the issue became increasingly controversial.

Georgia   Georgia proponents in general did not seek formal endorsements of the ERA from community leaders. However, Atlanta mayor Maynard Jackson endorsed it, as did the city councils and county commissions of Chatham and Savannah.[15]

Proponents received no help from the major politcal parties and leadership in Georgia. Said one supporter: "The [state] Republican party voted against ERA at last summer's meeting [1973] and the Democrats wouldn't touch it with a 10-foot pole." Legislators likewise recalled no contacts from party officials.

Governor Jimmy Carter came out in support of the ERA only after the 1973 legislative session. As one adherent explained:

> [He] had to fight for his political life so couldn't afford a controversial stance in 1973. He was pressured into a public stance and besides was a lame duck, so it couldn't hurt too much.

Even so, the governor's espousal proved to be a mixed blessing. In the fall of 1973, Carter revealed that his mail was running 9 to 1 against the ERA. "We've never been able to track down that figure, but it hurt us and we've never recovered," said a supporter. On another occasion, the governor told a delegation of opponents that although he supported the amendment, his wife opposed it. The next day Rosalynn Carter came to the capitol, wearing an "ERA Yes" button, and held a press conference, saying that her husband must have misunderstood her. For his part, Governor Carter saw the ERA as the type of issue on which a governor's influence is minimal. ("It's a relationship between the individual legislator and his hometown women.") His public statements thus were aimed less at influencing legislators than at activating proponent women to contact their own legislators. Quietly, the Governor met with legislators to persuade them to introduce the ERA, speak for it (or at least not speak against it), and vote for it.

Lieutenant Governor Lester Maddox was the one state official who might have served as a counterweight to the governor's support. Although opponents were aware of his public stand in opposition, proponents were able to extract a promise from him that, given an opportunity, he would only vote against it in the senate, but would not otherwise oppose it.

The Georgia Commission on the Status of Women was politically active for the first time as a member of the Statewide Coalition. Legislative members invariably recalled their contacts with the CSW, which published, at state expense, two brochures on the amendment, including a lengthy analysis of Georgia laws which might be affected by it. Despite criticism of these activities by opponents who felt that "the opposition to ERA should have equal representation on the Commission on the Status of Women," no legal action was taken.

Both female legislators in Georgia in 1974 spoke out for the ERA.[16] Opponents, however, did not interpret this as a disadvantage to their forces. Nor, apparently, could this allegiance be effectively used by proponents in the field. As one ERA supporter explained:

> I always told audiences that female legislators in Georgia supported ERA. But the fact that both are black means that in some parts of the state their endorsement doesn't carry much weight.

Pro-ERA groups did rely on these female legislators to influence other blacks in the house and the senate. One woman, an experienced and respected legislator, also served as an informal adviser to the Statewide Coalition.

Illinois   In 1974, a major effort was made by proponents in Illinois to collect endorsements for the ERA from a broad range of community and state leaders. In addition to a state ERA Week, proclaimed by Governor Daniel Walker, many mayors and village boards also proclaimed or passed pro-ERA resolutions. The executive committee of an ad hoc group formed by ERA Central, Men for the ERA, was quite impressive, listing names of newspaper publishers and columnists, industrialists, religious leaders, doctors, and attorneys. Politicians were well-represented also, among them both Illinois U.S. Senators, Chicago City Council members, Mayor Richard Daley, Governor Walker, and four other state elected officials.

Proponents, however, received few direct benefits from these endorsements in terms of heightened legislative support. According to one proponent:

> The community leaders are *for* ERA in Illinois—they're not avoiding a public stance. But they're not *working* for it. This isn't one of "their" issues.

Proponents were pleased with Governor Walker's vocal support,[17] but also acknowledged his limited influence in the legislature as an independent Democrat in deep conflict with the Chicago political machine. The so-called Daley votes in the legislature were evenly divided, a sign that the mayor had not put his clout behind the amendment. As one legislator phrased it in reference to all the high elected officials who formally support the ERA:

> Obviously this was not an issue that these men cared enough about to call in their political chips. This is the difference. It's not an issue that matters that much to them or else it would have passed.

Even though at least one mayor (in Springfield) declared a Stop ERA Week to coincide with Mother's Day, the Illinois opponents did not seek official statements of opposition, feeling instead that "this is strictly a women's movement." One adversary, however, asserted that there *were* prominent opponents in the state who preferred to remain anonymous. The comments of one legislative opponent would appear to confirm this:

> I haven't met many political, community, or business leaders who are for ERA. I've heard them *say* they were for it but then I

hear them in a personal sense . . . you'd be amazed at the political leaders' private statements about the women's lib movement, their comments concerning ERA.

Although the Illinois state political parties have not been actively involved in ratification, formal endorsements of the ERA have been made by the state Democratic Party as well as by key officers and clubs of both parties. As for those downstate Republican leaders who might be persuaded to publicly oppose the ERA, opposition women felt in 1974 that the "party is in such disrepute, that wouldn't help."

The Illinois Commission on the Status of Women has been less active on behalf of the ERA than have commissions in other states. It was, in fact, a member of ERA Central, but it included ERA material only within more general reports and thus avoided criticism from the opposition movement.

In Illinois, female legislators have served as the sponsors of the ERA in both houses and are recognized as its main proponents in floor debate.[18] Conversely, none of the female legislators who have voted against the ERA (one in each session 1972–75; five in 1977–78) has played a major role within the amendment opposition. Opposition groups have relied more heavily upon the negative reactions they see among male legislators directed toward their female colleagues:

——— [a female legislative opponent] was not nearly as effective for us as ——— [a female legislative supporter] was in taking her baby to the floor in a box. This was quite revolting. The last thing those men want is a crying baby.

The fact that its sponsors are women has helped the opponents. Men resent the females. Men and women are biologically different and women libbers have failed to recognize this.

Summary and Conclusions

This profile of the groups and individuals that became involved in ratification in the states indicates that both models of conflict are partially descriptive of the politics of ERA ratification.

Contrary to the community conflict model, established proponent groups did not withdraw from the debate nor did they become neutralized when conflict began. Instead, national groups in support of the ERA became even more active and better organized as the controversy thickened. State chapters of these groups also were active in support of the amendment in their state legislatures.

The community conflict model is more helpful for interpreting the group basis of ERA opposition. Ad hoc organizations were formed to this end, but many of their individual members, especially the leaders, were also members of previously existing national organizations on record as opposed to the amendment. While it would be incorrect to say that these latter groups withdrew or became neutralized, certain of their members apparently recognized that the public reputations of these established groups were not an asset. In hopes of presenting a more respectable image and of broadening their ideological appeal to the general public, members of such groups formed ad hoc organizations under which their other group affiliations were subsumed. Such groups, of course, could also attract the unaffiliated and dissenting members of proponent groups.

As expected, proponent organizations more nearly approximated the profile of the effective group, as described by the interest group conflict model, than did opposition groups. They were better-known in the community and more reputable than the opposing ad hoc organizations; they had large statewide memberships. In contrast stood small, narrowly partisan, groups such as Pro-America and the John Birch Society, from which the ad hoc opposition organizations drew their initial supporters. In terms of economic resources, proponent organizations in the states could bank upon their national organizations and their broad-based memberships as continuing sources of funding. Opposition ad hoc groups ostensibly depended solely on voluntary contributions from an ill-defined base of supporters.

Proponent groups in unratified states were generally successful in forming coalitions to coordinate their lobbying efforts. Because the pro-ERA coalition could claim to represent a diversified assortment of member-groups, rather than merely a collection of individuals as did the ad hoc opposition groups, proponents should have had a tactical advantage in their attempts to influence legislators. Such coalitions, in general, also exhibited more sophisticated organizational arrangements for planning, communications, lobbying, research, and public education than did their opposition counterparts.

The community conflict model correctly describes certain individuals who have become involved in the ERA controversy. The amendment has served to politicize many citizens at the grass-roots level who had had no previous experience with political activism. It would not be accurate, however, to characterize the leadership on either side as "low-status political amateurs." Most leaders were political amateurs only in the sense that relatively few were seasoned legislative lobbyists. Being primarily women, their experience more often was as political organizers and party workers. Those ERA activists who did have earlier lobbying experience, however, were more likely to be amendment supporters. In certain states, opposition leaders were also well-known political figures, usually through their association with the Republican Party or ultraconservative political groups such as the John Birch Society.

Nor could these leaders be considered "low-status" in terms of occupation or income. As has commonly been found in studies of elites, the group leaders closely resembled each other in status. Upper middle-class housewives and professional women acted as leaders on both sides of the issue. (One exception was the leadership of Happiness of Womanhood, which appeared to be a predominantly lower middle-class organization.) The status gap between the leadership and rank-and-file membership appeared to be smaller within proponent groups; "low-status political amateur" was more applicable to the constituency toward which the opposition channeled its public campaign.

Thus, the strongly upper middle-class participation assumed by the interest group conflict model was found here on both sides, although to a somewhat greater extent among proponents, who also were found to have an advantage in terms of past experience with legislative lobbying.

In addition to those active within groups working for the amendment, another source of support was found in community, state, and national leaders. On the national level, the President's family and staff and Labor Department employees involved with women's programs vigorously supported ERA ratification. And in the states, the extent of amendment support by community and state leaders seemed to depend primarily on how aggressively proponent organizations sought such assistance. Where it had been solicited, it was almost always given. Proponents, however, were invariably disappointed that only rarely was a formal statement of endorsement by these leaders accompanied by active lobbying among legislators on behalf of the ERA. While state and community leaders were not in so many words avoiding the issue, neither were they willing to assign the amendment's passage a high priority. The position of political parties in the states more closely approximated the neutrality described in the community conflict model. In some states, both parties remained aloof from the fray; in others, only one took a position.

Given the very different responses with which the ERA has met in the state legislatures, it was expected that there was some interstate variation in the composition of the groups and individuals that became involved in state ratification. This expectation was satisfied in the case studies.

Texas   In Texas, where the amendment was quickly ratified, no organized opposition existed at the time of ratification. Only a few proponents made any attempts to influence the legislature. The state's governor and its legislative leaders were firmly in support of ratification, as were both female legislators and the Texas Commission on the Status of Women. Aside from these key political figures, proponent groups did not seek further support from state and community leaders. Texas presents a pure example of the interest group model of conflict. In the absence of any countervailing opposition, only limited activity was needed to achieve ratification.

Georgia   In Georgia, where the amendment was soundly defeated, the proponents' claim to greater legitimacy was undercut by the participation of the Socialist Workers Party and a radical feminist group in an ad hoc pro-ERA organization. Although the opposition worked primarily through ad hoc groups under which established opposition groups were largely subsumed, opponents were perhaps less subject to a loss of legitimacy if their affiliation with far-right groups were publicized in a state carried by George Wallace in 1968 and where a national John Birch Society director was elected to Congress in 1974.

In general, the proponent groups were better organized than were the opposition groups. In comparison with pro-ERA coalitions in other nonratified states, however, the Georgia Statewide Coalition was lacking in method, funding, and member-group strength. Georgia proponents were advantaged in terms of political experience and elite support. According to the interest group model, despite organizational weaknesses and divisions among supporter groups, the advantages elsewhere should have been sufficient to assure greater support for the amendment in the legislature than was reflected in the floor votes. The community conflict model, then, may best describe the dynamics of ERA ratification in Georgia. The neutrality of the dominant Democratic party and the tardy endorsement of a lame-duck governor with Presidential ambitions are further indications of community conflict.

Illinois In Illinois, the legislature's sharp division on the ERA was reflected in the relative strengths and weaknesses of the interest groups in conflict over the issue. Neither side was clearly superior to the other.

ERA Central had a well-developed organizational structure, effective fund raising, and an extensive member-organization base. It attracted the support of leaders from many areas of public and private life. Its weaknesses, however, were major. By subsuming its member-organizations under ERA Central, the coalition was unable to profit from their separate strengths and well-established reputations. ERA Central, by depending upon its own staff for most of the active work of the legislative campaign, failed to involve many of the state's politically experienced amendment supporters.

Although outflanked in terms of organization and support from community and state leaders, the Illinois opposition was able to exploit the weakness in proponent leadership. The opponents were led by some unusually high-status and politically experienced women, and, contrary to the situation in other states, the leadership was not restricted to persons with right-wing affiliations. Even those women identified chiefly with far-right associations were able to use their alliance with the conservative wing of the state Republican party to good advantage in their anti-ERA activities.

Except for the appearance of several ad hoc groups, ERA ratification in Illinois would be a classic interest group conflict between two strong opposing forces. Taken together, however, the group, individual, and elite bases of alignment on the ERA in Illinois suggest an admixture of both models of conflict.

NOTES

1. Irene L. Murphy, "Strategy for Ratification of the Equal Rights Amendment: A Political Science Model Applied to a Practical Situation," paper delivered at the 1974 Annual Spring Conference of the National Capitol Area Political Science Association, American University, Washington, D.C., 27 April 1974.
2. John G. Schmitz, "Look Out: They're Planning to Draft Your Daughter," *American Opinion* 15 (November 1972): 1–16.
3. *John Birch Society Bulletin*, February 1973, p. 25.
4. Lisa Cronin Wohl, "Phyllis Schlafly: The Sweetheart of the Silent Majority," *Ms.* 2 (March 1974): 87.
5. Quoted in *National Catholic Reporter*, 16 February 1973.
6. *Women Today* 3 (5 February, 1973): 6.
7. Ann K. Justice, ed., *The Insurance Connection with Stop ERA Forces* (Lincoln, Nebr.: Lincoln NOW, 1974). There has been much speculation that segments of the insurance industry are concerned that their sex-differentiated practices might come under severe scrutiny if the ERA were passed. These include disability insurance for which women pay as much as 150 percent more than men; and pension plans, which commonly yield women lower benefits than men, based on their longer life expectancy.
8. The Texas Equal Legal Rights Amendment was first introduced in the legislature in 1959 and was finally passed in the regular session of 1971. It was approved by the voters in November 1972 (after ERA ratification in Texas) by a margin of 4–1.
9. It is the opinion of most legal experts, including the Department of Justice in a 1977 opinion, that a state cannot rescind its previous approval of a constitutional amendment. According to them, the Constitution only gives the states the power to ratify an amendment.

The Supreme Court, in its only ruling on the subject, *Coleman* v. *Miller*, 307 U.S. 433 (1939), has declared that rescission is a political question to be decided by Congress. And in the past, Congress has refused to honor rescission resolutions. However, these congressional actions occurred more than a century ago and opponents of the ERA in many ratifying states have vigorously pursued moves to rescind. For two legal commentaries on this question see: Raymond M. Planell, "The Equal Rights Amendment: Will States Be Allowed to Change Their Minds?" *Notre Dame Lawyer* 49 (February 1974): 657–70; J. William Heckman, Jr., "Ratification of a Constitutional Amendment: Can a State Change Its Mind?" *Connecticut Law Review* 6 (1973): 28–35.

10. This was also the heading of an early *Phyllis Schlafly Report* (November 1972) discussing the ERA.
11. See: Maren Lockwood Carden, *The New Feminist Movement* (New York: Russell Sage Foundation, 1974); Carolyn Stoloff, "Who Joins Women's Liberation?" *Psychiatry* 36 (August 1973): 325–40; Catherine Arnott, "Feminists and Anti-Feminists as 'True Believers,'" *Sociology and Social Research* 57 (April 1973): 300–306.
12. For two studies of the backgrounds and political attitudes of participants in the anti-ERA movement in a single state, see David W. Brady and Kent L. Tedin, "Ladies in Pink: Religion and Political Ideology in the Anti-ERA Movement," *Social Science Quarterly* 56 (March 1976): 564–75; Theodore S. Arrington and Patricia A. Kyle, "Equal Rights Amendment Activists in North Carolina," paper delivered at the Annual Meeting of the American Political Science Association, San Francisco, September 1975.
13. Lawrence D. Longley, "Interest Group Interactions in a Legislative System," *Journal of Politics* 29 (August 1967): 637–58.
14. Although the governor of Texas determines which bills will be considered in a special session, joint resolutions *may* be taken up by either house without the governor's authorization.
15. In 1977, a number of prominent Georgia politicians' wives endorsed the ERA at a senate luncheon. Included were Rosalynn Carter, Betty Talmadge, state First Lady Mrs. George Busbee, and Mrs. Sam Nunn.
16. Although only 2 women served in the Georgia legislature, 1973–74, 12 women were elected to the state legislature in November 1974 and again in 1976.
17. Republican Governor James Thompson, elected in 1976, also endorsed the ERA in a message to the legislature in June 1977. Earlier in the year, however, he promised to leave the fate of the ERA to the legislature, despite a campaign pledge to actively work for the amendment.
18. In 1972 there were only 4 women in the Illinois legislature. Female representation increased in successive legislatures to: 11 (1973–74), 14 (1975–76), and 21 (1977–78).

4 The Lobbying Campaign

In almost every state that has considered ratification of the Equal Rights Amendment since January 1973, the amendment has been an "important legislative issue."[1] It has attracted the attention of interest groups and of legislators as well as the notice of each state's governor and of the media. Many previously politically inactive citizens have also been drawn into the controversy. The individual legislator thus has been subjected to both external and internal pressures: He or she received messages from organized groups, constituents, the media, and perhaps even direct contacts from the governor concerning the ERA; and where legislative cleavages existed, coercion often was applied to adhere to the position taken on the subject by one's party, faction, or geographical locality.

In this chapter, the external pressures upon the legislators are considered through an examination of the strategies and tactics used by both proponent and opponent groups. The particular problems of women as lobbyists are noted.

Gaining Public Support and Expanding the Conflict

The value of public opinion and grass-roots support in influencing legislators is widely recognized by groups engaged in traditional interest group politics. In the case of the ERA, an effective proponent group must convince legislators that it represents the opinion of *all* women on the issue and that the amendment's potential impact is consistent with societal values generally. Opposition groups must convey the impression that *they* are most representative of women and the public at large and that their position is most consonant with existing social attitudes.

In community conflicts, as contrasted with interest group conflicts, inclusion of the public at large in the controversy is particularly crucial. At its height, a community conflict will have involved a high percentage of a given population, if not actively, at least as interested and aware observers. To attract this broader participation, new and different points become introduced and the original disputed issues are redefined, simplified, and often distorted. Beyond this, the media play a distinct role in broadening the conflict.

Public Opinion Polls

Amendment proponents have frequently used national polls in their attempts to show that they and their groups are representative of local, state, and national opinion on the ERA. Granted, a national poll may be discounted by a legislator if it says nothing about attitudes in his/her district. Even so, ERA supporters consider it impressive that every poll taken from 1974 through 1977 has indicated that a majority of the American public supports "the proposed Equal Rights Amendment." (Table 4.1 gives a profile of the demographic base of ERA support.)

Efforts to measure public opinion on the ERA within a single state or local area have all reaffirmed that it is endorsed by a majority of citizens. Ball State University researchers in 1974 found a 70 percent majority for the amendment in Indiana. A poll conducted in 1974 by the *Prairie Farmer Magazine* found that farm women in Indiana and Illinois supported it, 2 to 1. At a Missouri senate hearing on the ERA in 1974, an independent poll taker reported that 60 percent of Missourians polled favored it and, in another sampling, 80 percent approved the amendment's wording.[2] A survey by the Jackson *Clarion Ledger* in 1973 showed that a

TABLE 4.1
Support for the Equal Rights Amendment

	Favor	Oppose	No Opinion
National	57%	24%	19%
Sex			
Male	59	23	18
Female	55	26	19
Race			
White	56	26	18
Nonwhite	60	13	27
Education			
College	65	24	11
High School	54	26	20
Grade School	51	23	26
Region			
East	58	22	20
Midwest	56	26	18
South	53	26	21
West	61	24	15
Age			
18–29 years	64	18	18
30–49 years	56	26	18
50 and older	52	28	20
Party Identification			
Republican	54	28	18
Democrat	56	24	20
Independent	60	23	17
Religion			
Protestant	54	27	19
Catholic	58	23	19
Occupation			
Professional and Business	59	24	17
Clerical and Sales	58	28	14
Manual Workers	59	22	19
Not in Labor Force	·55	25	20

TABLE 4.1
Support for the Equal Rights Amendment (*Cont.*)

	Favor	Oppose	No Opinion
Population of Residence			
1,000,000 and over	60	21	19
500,000–999,999	61	19	20
50,000–499,999	60	25	15
2,500–49,999	54	29	17
Under 2,500, Rural	51	27	22
Marital Status			
Married	54	28	18
Single	64	15	21

SOURCE: "Women in America," *Gallup Opinion Index 128* (March 1976), p. 18.

majority of Mississippi voters wanted the ERA ratified. And an Illinois proponent cited a countywide poll taken in 1974 by an ultraconservative downstate newspaper which indicated a 60 percent majority for the ERA.

Opponents of the amendment, as well, have used public opinion polls in their campaign. Instead of directly measuring opinion on the ERA, however, these polls probe reactions to its potential impact. A 1971 Roper Poll which was read into the *Congressional Record* by Senator Sam Ervin is widely quoted by the opposition.[3] It indicates that a majority of the American public were hostile to the notions of men receiving alimony on the basis of need or equal treatment for women in the military draft. However, equal pay and equal job opportunities for women *were* strongly supported. Interspersed among these questions were items related to several of the prospective ERA "horrors" such as admitting women to membership in private men's clubs and lodges, role reversal ("the wife should be the breadwinner if a better wage earner than the husband"), and sex-integrated football teams. Majorities were found in opposition to all these latter practices.

Perhaps more significant, a Gallup Poll taken in March 1976 found that 90 percent of the respondents said they had read or heard about "the Equal Rights Amendment to the Constitution which would give women equal rights and equal responsibilities." At any rate, the ERA had captured a wide audience.

Public Education

ERA proponents attempted a public education campaign only after the amendment encountered opposition in the state legislatures. The feeling was that if the ERA could be explained and grass-roots enthusiasm for it engendered, legislators would then vote according to their constituents' wishes. Therefore, shortly after the legislative defeats, coalitions in unratified states began setting up speakers bureaus and scheduling forums and workshops around the state.

In Texas, there was neither time nor need for grass-roots education by groups supporting the ERA. But in both Georgia and Illinois such an approach was tried. In Illinois, letter writing was encouraged through appearances by members of the ERA Central Speakers Bureau. Letter-writing booths were also set up in shopping centers in the Chicago area. In Georgia, the Statewide Coalition encouraged grass-roots education through open meetings of their groups. NOW and G-ERA focused their main efforts on demonstrations, forums, and workshops. But, as a leader of BPW in Georgia explained,

> Grass-roots education was only "tried" and that is one reason why it failed in Georgia. I assumed that there couldn't be a woman living who was against the ERA. And when this opposition developed, we just didn't have the time to carry on the education we should have. It was misinformation which defeated the ERA in Georgia.

Leaders of the opposition from the beginning addressed themselves to creating a grass-roots movement, because it was needed in order to compete with the stronger organizations favoring the amendment. Commenting upon the ratification by Maine and Montana in early 1974, the *John Birch Society Bulletin* stated: "This was not due, however, to apathy on the part of our members in those states, but to the circumstances that there are so few of them." [4] The first project of the

National Committee to Restore Women's Rights was a direct-mail campaign to various women's groups in Texas, explaining the ERA's feared impact and asking the women to contact their legislators. Opposition leaders in Georgia asserted that their basic goal was public education: "People-to-people contacts are the only effective tactic, not group-to-group like proponents." Opposition women in Illinois, too, emphasized mass mailings and appearances before small groups. According to one opponent in Illinois, they relied on the "natural revulsion from the grass roots which is inherent in *all* women."[5]

The public education campaign of both proponents and opponents followed the pattern of traditional interest group politics in so far as each was aimed primarily at activating people to write letters or otherwise contact their legislators in behalf of the ERA. The literature and other information provided by proponents on the subject dealt with the amendment's legal impact as interpreted in congressional documents and law review articles. This approach is again that of providing expertise within the interest group conflict model.

The parallel attempts by opponents to broaden their base of support, however, seemed to follow the pattern of previous community conflicts. The opposition has not always restricted itself to the merits and demerits of the ERA itself. Instead, new and distinct issues, logically unrelated to the amendment, were interjected into the debate. Some, such as abortion, were subjects on which the community was already divided; with the introduction of these new bases of emotional response, new participants and supporters were brought into the anti-ERA movement. Others, such as the sanctity of the home, were introduced which allowed for a response in only one direction. Finally, the debate itself became weighted down in inflammatory language, expressing virulent animosity toward amendment supporters. The following excerpts, taken from opposition literature, are illustrative:

> [On protective labor laws.] A woman called me from a major corporation to tell me they had lost all their protective laws. She said they used to have a chair to sit on when they were not working. That's gone now. They used to get extra rest breaks. Those are gone now. They could call a man to lift anything very

heavy. Now they have to lift it themselves. They are being forced into men's jobs. She said, "Jaquie, they are literally killing us. It's nothing to see a six-months pregnant woman digging in a pit."[6]

[On family support.] This means that, if the husband is lazy and wants to drink beer and watch television all day and the wife is a conscientious woman who takes a job to feed her hungry children, then she, as the "principal wage-earning spouse," would acquire the *obligation* to support her lazy husband, subject to criminal penalties if she failed to support him and pay all his debts![7]

[On family life.] The amendment would simply dynamite the natural foundation of marriage and our traditional family life. It would consign married women to the same unhappy predicament of unwed or deserted mothers, by lifting from husbands and fathers any special obligation to support their families. It would be certain to increase, rather than decrease, public dependency—this at a time when the responsible members of society, who *do* support their families, are groaning under the burden of providing (through taxation) for millions of "fatherless" children and their mothers!

It would also *force* married women to leave their home and children for work by making them just as responsible for "bringing home the bacon" as their husbands and by making them provide for their own declining years.[8]

[On military service for women.] . . . when girls are killed in action, they will get the same death benefits as the men do. When girls have their arms and legs shot off, they, too, will get disabled veterans' benefits. And when they are taken prisoners of war, they will share in all the "benefits" of being a POW, equally with men, if they are released.[9]

[On privacy.] Does it make you feel strange to learn that the only thing between you ladies and leering strangers of the opposite sex is *Griswold* v. *Connecticut*? My wife says she would prefer a wall.[10]

[On equal rights in Russia.] "Equal rights" in the Soviet Union means that the Russian woman is obliged to put her baby in a state-operated nursery or kindergarten so she can join the labor force. "Equal rights" in Russia means that the women do the heavy, dirty work American women do not do—but men are still the bosses.[11]

[On the women's liberation movement.] The women's libbers are radicals who are waging a total assault on the family, on marriage, and on children.[12]

[On the National Organization for Women.] . . . the way out, radical fringe group which is leading the battle for ERA, namely, the National Organization of [sic] Women. . . . When they talk to themselves in their own publications, they reveal their revolutionary objectives. Their own platform of principles is appropriately titled *Revolution: Tomorrow is NOW*.[13]

Ms. Schlafly in her *Reports* has also attempted to link the amendment with pornography, *Ms.* magazine, women in non-traditional careers (e.g., prison guard, policeworker,[14] and sailor), and abortion.

Of these various "side-issues," three have been of particular significance in the states studied here.

The women's liberation movement has been widely associated with the ERA in the minds of certain sectors of the public and the legislature. Governor Jimmy Carter, analyzing the 1974 defeat in Georgia, commented in a personal interview:

> There's been some confusion between ERA as such and the Women's Liberation people. Instead of looking at ERA as a way to guarantee women equal employment opportunities, they look on it as a movement by the Gay Liberation Front or Gloria Steinem and other more liberal and exotic characters to destroy proper relationships between husbands and wives.

In heavily Catholic Illinois, abortion has been a leading peripheral subject. In 1974, two mailings were sent by opponents to church leaders in the state in an attempt to link the ERA with the proabortion movement. As one proponent observed:

> Conservative opponents have been able to convince people that rights for women and rights for fetuses are incompatible. Not all people believe that—and members of ERA Central are also members of the Right-to-Life Committee—but in the minds of some people and in the minds of a good number of Catholic Church leaders, we have a situation where they truly believe that to give women equal legal rights will destroy the family and will lead to a widespread decline in morality, and will ulti-

mately lead to abortion. And there is nothing in this world that is going to change that.

Only in Georgia was the ERA seriously discussed as subversive or communist in nature. One opposition group leader cautiously said, "I won't say ERA is a conspiracy against the government but right now it looks very much like it is." Others were more outspoken, quoting Lenin, Engels, Marx, Trotsky, and even Fidel Castro on the "liberation of women" and "equal rights." Inadvertently, G-ERA strengthened opponents' suspicions concerning a linkage between communism and the ERA by using the cropped cover of *Feminism and Socialism*, a book published by the Socialist Workers Party, on one of their ERA flyers.

Despite the feeling of many ERA supporters that these opposition interpretations of the amendment were not worthy of serious response, it soon became apparent that, however inaccurate and outlandish, they were effective. Jean McCarrey, president of BPW, admitted that these arguments were succeeding with "dependent wives, who have no identity outside the family and fear that ERA will threaten their status, and with men for whom equal rights for women is seen as a threat to their masculinity."[15]

ERA opponents did not need to actually prove that the amendment would have the impact they envisioned; they needed only to generate doubt in the minds of the general public. Supporters, in responding to opposition rhetoric, succeeded only in further confusing the public and raising the level of controversy. After the opposition mobilized, ERA proponents were perforce placed on the defensive, arguing *against* the straw men and red herrings of their adversaries, rather than *for* the positive aspects of the amendment. And in countering these allegations, supporters found themselves resorting to complex explanations of the law and comparing statistics not readily grasped by the layperson. Ironically, such public information programs can even have the effect of reversing favorable dispositions.

The opposition of churches and individual religious leaders has also proven to be a problem in almost every unratified state for those seeking to rally public support behind the ERA. The Church of Jesus Christ of Latter-Day Saints (Mormon) has taken an official stand against the ERA on the grounds that men and women have different roles in society. This pronouncement has doomed the amendment in Utah's predominantly Mormon legislature and is felt to be influential also in the neighboring state of Nevada, which has a sizable Morman population. Although fundamentalist Protestant churches, in the absence of a central hierarchy, have not taken official positions in opposition to the amendment, many observers feel that legislators in the Deep South (and to a lesser extent in the Midwestern states) are reflecting fundamentalist religious views on women's role in their rejection of the ERA. This view is reflected in an essay by a Georgia Independent Baptist minister and in a verse, "Pray for the Defeat of ERA," which was distributed to Indiana legislators:

> God clearly created male and female as different and distinct, though both are equally human. Thus, to deny the difference is to deny reality, but, more than that, to deny the Word of God. (I would point out here that I believe this is the essence of ERA. It is a denial of God, both as to His person and to His program and purposes for mankind.)[16]

> That the ERA takes from women
> Those rights assigned to them by Thee
> The right to be just a wife and mother
> The right to give up rights for Thee.[17]

It is admittedly difficult to attack a political opinion based on sincerely held religious beliefs. Furthermore, this kind of religious censure has been especially formidable in that it associates opposition to the ERA with deeply held societal values relating to home, motherhood, and God.

The Role of the Media

The media have played an important role in the struggle over ERA ratification. Attracted by the confrontational aspects of the ERA controversy, the media have frequently jointly featured the two opposing sides. Although no precise figures are available on the number of newspapers which have taken an editorial position on the matter, in general, many major metropolitan newspapers have tended to support the ERA while the smaller dailies and weeklies have not. Significantly, it is the newspapers in the nonratifying or late-ratifying states (where conflict has been highest) which have most often taken editorial stands. While media coverage may heighten the level of conflict, such conflict probably does not originate with the media. Rather is it the existing conflict which eventually forces most major newspapers to take a position.

Despite the different legislative responses with which the ERA has met in the states studied, there was apparently a surprising degree of unanimity on two points concerning the media. Proponents as a rule were pleased with media coverage and saw it as a useful tool for educating the public and influencing legislators. Opponents reported media distortion and personal abuse at the hands of the media. Though, according to the community conflict model, what is said in the media is less important than the fact that an argument is in progress, this was not the perception of either side.

Texas   As was largely true of the media in quickly ratifying states, the Texas media took no position on the ERA in 1972, but proponents invariably praised them for their "fairness." In general, pro-ERA groups reported receiving publicity in all media for their views and activities.

The late-mobilizing opposition in Texas was not nearly so successful. A spokesperson for the National Committee to Restore Women's Rights complained in 1974:

> Texas media coverage on ERA has been very little. We have put out many many press releases, none of which were included in a major newspaper. We got television time under the Fairness Doctrine, but at 8:30 a.m. Sunday, with only two exceptions. The media probably are not consciously suppressing us but they are suppressing us.

Illinois   In Illinois, the media took a more active role. According to one of ERA's legislative sponsors, the amendment received statewide coverage and, to her knowledge, none of the media was in opposition. Chicago-area proponents also claimed to have media contacts for "planting" items in columns and for getting news stories included as well.

ERA opponents in Illinois, however, voiced many complaints against the media. These included inability to get coverage through press releases and slanted stories, selectively edited. The opposition has made a real effort to use the media through letters to the editor, countereditorials, and

TV/radio talk show appearances. Yet they conceded that a serious weakness of their movement is their relative inexperience in media use as compared with the amendment proponents, many of whom are in the communications field.

Georgia   The situation in Georgia roughly paralleled that in Illinois. In general, ERA supporters felt the media were very fair to both sides. Although the Atlanta papers did endorse the amendment, they did so only one week before the 1974 house vote. In turn, Georgia opponents of the ERA voiced complaints similar to those of their counterparts in other states.

However, both sides leveled strong criticism against the media on one point: It was agreed that the media selected unrepresentative spokespersons for both sides. "The liberal media appointed J. B. Stoner as *the* antispokesman," complained one amendment opponent, but this was rectified when members of the opposition protested. Members of the Statewide Coalition in turn charged:

> The electronic media did nothing but disservice to ERA proponents. The ERA was always equated with NOW or lesbians and with equal time they always used NOW people, which reinforced this. The League of Women Voters, BPW, AAUW were *never* mentioned. Instead, the media wanted to use more activist groups as the spokespersons. They asked loaded questions of women and in general tried to put groups at each others' throats.

Assuming these criticisms to be valid, it would appear that the media in Georgia played a role in expanding conflict over the ERA by choosing to stress the least moderate elements of both movements. The debate format initially used by the local Atlanta television stations also widened the controversy in that discussion became highly emotional. At the request of a BPW leader, however, a policy of "separate but equal" time allotment was later adopted by these stations.

The media are not an ally to be undervalued in a campaign to influence public policy, as is illustrated by the comments of one Illinois legislator, a vocal amendment opponent:

> Most important is the media and the women have the four major Chicago papers riding the ERA bandwagon. It's difficult for some legislators to resist because all want to cozy up to the

media. Those of us who oppose the ERA have been painted by the media as Neanderthal chauvinists or as "just dumb" and "not with it." They fail to give us any credit for legal scholarship or sensitivity to women's rights.

Tactics and Strategies of ERA Partisans

Participants in both traditional interest group politics and community conflicts place great emphasis on attracting support among the general public, whether through grassroots education or the media, as has been seen. Those engaging in interest group politics, however, are more concerned with the specific tactics and strategies used to influence decision makers than are participants in community conflicts. As is typical of those following the "insider" strategy, participants in traditional interest group politics closely adhere to the established rules of political lobbying (i.e., avoiding the use of disruptive and other unsanctioned tactics). In community conflicts, unconventional tactics are commonly adopted since many participants are "outsiders," unconstrained by the political rules of the game.

Women as Lobbyists

Political scientists have only rarely considered women's groups in the context of political participation. Women, in general, have been portrayed in the literature as a categorical group with few common political interests. It is felt that women's groups lack unity on concrete policies and therefore are of little political consequence.[18] In this respect, the ERA ratification campaign has been unusual in that it is women's groups who have been almost exclusively involved in lobbying on both sides of the issue.[19] The ERA conflict thus presents an opportunity to consider the relationship between the lobbyist's gender and access, tactics, and impact.[20]

Supporting earlier findings concerning the reception of the League of Women Voters by Congress,[21] female lobbyists agreed that, as females, they received a courteous hearing from almost all legislators. As one Illinois proponent put it:

_____ [an outspoken opponent] is just all charm; he's a "lady's man." The opponents are often the *most* courteous because they have this notion of the southern gentleman: Be nice to a lady just because she's a lady.

But underneath this surface courtliness may lie a fear of women or women's groups or both. Lyndon Johnson was reported to have once said, "I like women singly but I am afraid of them in groups."[22] Or, as a vocal legislative opponent of the amendment in Georgia explained:

> We're more afraid of some of these women's groups than we are of men's groups because they can really build up an organization against you and really tear you apart in the Capitol. It's hard to get around some of these women's organizations. You can't talk to them as rough as you can to these men.

One problem faced by women's groups in their attempt to influence legislators may stem from their exclusion from the common socio-occupational pool from which state legislators and lobbyists are drawn.[23] Though female lobbyists may closely resemble legislators in *level* of education, women in the United States continue to experience educational and occupational phenomena very different from those of men. State legislators, for example, most commonly list law or business as their occupation. Yet only a few independent businesswomen were engaged in direct lobbying for or against the ERA. And even more rarely were female lawyers found in this role, despite their activities as legal advisors, hearings witnesses, and public speakers. Thus female lobbyists rarely were able to benefit from a special rapport with legislators stemming from a shared occupational background.

Additionally women's groups, in particular those supporting the amendment, are strongly associated in the legislators' minds with reformist measures and a public interest orientation. Legislators, faced with the harsh realities of political survival and forced daily to balance competing interests, may tend to dismiss women's groups such as the League of Women Voters as impractical "lady-do-gooders." Appeals to consider the general welfare in policy making only increase a legislator's internal conflicts.[24] Legislators are felt to give greater weight to groups acting in their own self-interest. ERA opponents have structured their arguments along very personal lines—the home and family.[25] Proponents, conversely, have relied upon such broad general interest concepts as "equality," "justice under law," "equity," and "right." Even when proponents have attempted to tie the issue to home and family, they have encountered difficulties as females. A Vermont supporter complained:

> It's "Catch-22." If you argue in an emotional way, they say you're "only a woman." If you debate logically and effectively, they say you're too mannish. After some of our wives and mothers testified for the amendment, the gossip around the State House the next day was that they were fakes. They couldn't have been *real* mothers because they spoke too well.[26]

The fact that most of those active in ERA ratification have been women has also had an effect on tactics. Amendment proponents, in particular, have been very conscious of dress style. They were conscious of the association of the ERA in the minds of many legislators with the more militant elements of the new feminist movement, and had also observed the emphasis placed upon traditional femininity by the opposition campaign. As a result, ERA supporters often found themselves trying to "out-lady" opponents. A coalition leader in Missouri warned, "I will personally scalp any woman who shows up at the capitol building in pants or boots."[27] A "ladylike" appearance became the norm as proponents became increasingly anxious to try *any* tactic which might hasten ratification. This spirit of pragmatism was voiced by NOW's legislative vice-president, the late Ann Scott: "If it takes white gloves, we'll use white gloves. If it takes combat boots, we'll wear combat boots. If it takes white gloves and combat boots, we'll use both."[28]

A leader of G-ERA reported that she had bought new clothes for capitol and media appearances. Another proponent, active in the Illinois ERA Central Speakers Bureau, explained her personal strategy this way:

> You end up being as ladylike as you can, as sweet, as charming. You get your hair fixed on the days you speak for the ERA and you wear your ERA dress wardrobe.

Apparently this strategy has been successful in some states. In Maine, after ratification in 1974, an opposition leader complained that the proponent women had softened their approach that year: "They came on phony. They didn't come and lobby in blue jeans and they were soft-spoken."[29]

The General Legislative Campaign

Despite these particular dilemmas faced by women as lobbyists, both proponents and opponents of the ERA have in general organized their campaigns as would any other interest group—by determining the position of each legislator on the issue (doing headcounts), personal lobbying, and providing testimony and supplementary information on the amendment. One stratagem in particular which has distinguished the ERA ratification campaign is mass political letter writing. This is not an unusual method; Americans have long considered personal communication of their views to elected officials as a right and occasionally a duty.[30] But the volume of mail received on this issue has been exceptional.

The opposition has been particularly accomplished at this maneuver. One Illinois opponent stated that she had women who were "committed to sending ten letters a day to certain legislators we're concentrating on." And after Ms. Schlafly went to Atlanta in 1973 to testify against the ERA, mail to Georgia legislators suddenly began running 10 to 1 in opposition.

Letter writing is particularly appropriate and effective for the opposition movement. Political mail traditionally has been a means through which largely unorganized and transitory interests could articulate their demands. Only a minimum level of literacy and verbal ability is required to write a brief letter, relative to the more specialized skills (as well as poise and self-confidence) needed for personal contacts with legislators. Letter writing can be done in the home, at one's discretion—ideal conditions for the housewife antagonistic to the ERA who wants to "do something." Furthermore, the tendency of letter writers to send mail only when they think their "side" is losing (but not when they are confident of victory) provided at least an initial advantage to amendment opponents. Proponents admittedly had been reassured by the ratifications of 22 states in 1972 and were unprepared to launch a forceful campaign when the opposition emerged in 1973. Finally, mail per se, regardless of the precise division of opinion, is often regarded as a "storm warning" by legislators who may wait for the deluge to cease before disposing of the issue. At a minimum, a mail campaign assures closer scrutiny of the proposed legislation.

In their eagerness to swell the mailbags, opposition forces have availed themselves of two rather dubious expedients: writing to legislators in states other than their own and "inventing" constituents. A February 21, 1975, article in the *Arizona Republic* reported that one representative had discovered that more than half his anti-ERA mail came from people who did not exist. After his announcement, other legislators revealed that many of their responses to anti-ERA letters were being returned "no such address, no such person."

Although it is generally felt that legislators give more weight to unorganized than to organized mail if it arrives in comparable quantity, they do not totally discount form letters, hand-copied or reproduced, since they do indicate interest on the part of citizens. Even if coming from out-of-state or from nonexistent individuals, the letters do represent considerable effort, expense, and, presumably, concern on the part of *someone*. Proponents have come to realize that a major legislative yardstick for measuring support for and opposition to the ERA has been the quantity, not quality (or even authenticity), of letters received. In regard to at least this one tactic of traditional interest group politics, it is the opponents of the ERA who have been most successful in conveying the impression that they are representative of majority opinions.

In the use of other common interest group logistics, however, proponents have demonstrated superiority. One characteristic of the effective interest group is its focus upon key persons in the legislative process: the leadership, committee members, the undecided. If, however, the issue is very important to the group and the legislative vote is expected to be very close, each legislator will be contacted, preferably by his/her own constituents. Group positions on the issue will be presented in terms consonant with legislative and societal values. Above all, an effective interest group is active and will frequently interact with decision makers.

The general tone of this phase of the proponents' campaign is illustrated by the 80-page "ERA Campaign Countdown Kit" produced by the League of Women Voters. It contains sobersided advice on campaign timing, headcounting, legislative coordination, lobbying, testifying, and monitoring the opposition. Also included is a fact sheet on the amendment's potential impact entitled "Cool Facts for the Hot-Headed Opposition."

In stark contrast stands the lobbying strategy outlined by one of the leaders (male) of the opposition movement in Florida in a frank interview published in the *Miami Herald*, March 22, 1974. His opening move, he explained, was to use a "startling statement" on homosexuals, restrooms, or military combat to catch the legislator's attention:

> The startling statement must garner the customer's, or in this case the legislator's, attention. You don't go into a lot of details and ramifications. You get directly into a gut issue, expound on it and shut up. Once you've got their attention, then you can get into serious discussion of the issue.

He also expressed a preference for seizing upon the most visible group in the pro-ERA coalition, the National Organization for Women, and making them ("hairy-chested, no-bra women's libbers") the issue, rather than the ERA.

To the extent that this approach is followed by opponents, the legislative campaigns closely resemble that waged among the general public. Again, the original issues surrounding the ERA undergo major transformation in order to attract additional support.

Texas   In Texas, only a few women and women's groups —all supporters—attempted to influence legislators on the ERA at the time of ratification. Even fewer individuals went to Austin, the capital, to lobby personally. But even here, attempts were made in 1972 to encourage constituent communication with legislators. One woman contacted the legislative leadership and Governor Preston Smith, asking that the ERA be taken up in the March 1972 special session. She sent telegrams urging ratification of the amendment to every legislator and spoke directly with potential floor debate participants. As for organized opposition, as has been noted, there was none. A spokesperson for the John Birch Society noted he was not even aware that the ERA was being taken up at the special session. He continued:

> There wasn't any alert made at this stage to do something about it. We just slipped up there, I will admit. We didn't really realize what it was, or at least I didn't.

Georgia   Georgia supporters of the amendment, after the formal split in 1973, in effect waged two legislative campaigns: one with a more visible, vocal, and aggressive grassroots approach and another with a lower-key, legislator-centered approach. Before that time, the strategy had been to maintain the ERA at a very low profile, removed from the public eye. From the summer of 1972 to January 1973, proponents had worked quietly for passage only to see the amendment put into a special study committee in the house until the 1974 session. Even after that setback, the Statewide Coalition adhered to its understated strategy aimed at restricting the level of public controversy as much as possible. In the more activist groups' view, though, the ERA was being kept in committee only because the legislators never felt they had to answer to their constituents. One way to remedy that was to *raise* the level of controversy by public demonstrations of support for the ERA.

All agreed, however, that the first priority was getting the amendment out of committee in 1974. A four-month letter and phone-call campaign directed at the 13-person committee was launched by the Statewide Coalition and all other groups. Proponents wanted a recorded vote so they could pin down every legislator. ("They tell us one thing and ten minutes later tell the John Birch Society something else.")

With the exception of G-ERA, all supporting groups relied upon their members to convince the legislators in their own districts to approve the amendment. They were very much aware that legislators can easily dismiss the demands of women who fail to vote for them. Both the GWPC and NOW had a statewide lobbying network, although a spokesperson of NOW candidly admitted that up until the final month her group rarely contacted individual legislators. "Other more

traditional women's groups were doing that, were more experienced in doing that, and probably were better received
than NOW would have been."

Unquestionably, the Statewide Coalition had the more
elaborate lobbying network. Personal phone calls were placed
over WATS lines to members of the local Human Relations
Commission, Common Cause, and Coalition member-groups.
These people were asked to find five to ten others to phone
and visit local representatives and to see that 15 to 20 pro-
ERA letters were received by each legislator in a given
district.

One supporter conceded that this approach should have
been initiated much earlier; it was implemented on a large
scale only in November 1973. Thus the Coalition was forced to
concentrate on its strongest areas, neglecting areas where
adamant opponents resided or where it had no or only weak
local contacts. Even so, the persons in the districts disbursed
accurate information on legislative positions; the Statewide
Coalition's headcount on the day of the house floor vote was
within one vote of the actual tally.

In recalling their approaches and the issues they stressed in
attempting to enlist legislators on their behalf, most Georgia
proponents recounted some variation of the theme that women
needed to be protected under the U.S. Constitution. One, however, responded in a manner which captured much of the
frustration proponents felt in participating in a campaign
which was suddenly converted into an irrational, ideology-
tinged conflict:

> The arguments I used varied with the legislator. Some you can
> talk to intelligently, give them the facts and materials, give them
> time to digest it, and come back and answer questions. Some
> you have to appeal to emotionally; that's the approach that
> most of us took this year [1974]. I think that's a mistake a lot of us
> made in 1973 because we went into it with a lot of very rational,
> logical, common sense types of approaches. We figured the other
> people out here would do their emotional thing, but because we
> were intelligent and had a lot of common sense, we'd win out in the
> end, which is not true.... So a lot of us started to come on strong with
> things like, "How can you be against equality?" or "How can you
> deny women the right to be included in the Constitution?" and silly
> stuff like that. To me it's silly but to them it made sense. And with
> some it worked and you just had to judge.

As ERA supporters remember, the opposition manifested itself in Georgia the first weekend after the legislature convened in January 1973. The legislature and the entire state were flooded with reams of anti-ERA literature. As one supporter described it:

> The opposition did not begin in Georgia at the grass-roots. It was stimulated by outside agitators from Florida, Arizona, Illinois, and Ohio—Schlafly's people. The mail originally came from out-of-state. . . . The anti-ERA leaders in Georgia weren't the type of people you'd expect to get involved.

Contrary to the natural tendency for leaders to attribute to their groups greater skills, techniques, and organization than actually may be the case, opposition leaders in Georgia, if anything, emphasized their movement's weaknesses. No particular attempt was made to keep the resolution in committee by concentrating efforts on the Special Judiciary Committee. Several groups reported statewide petition drives, a tactic costly in time and energy that is generally conceded to have only marginal impact upon legislators. Although local members of HOW, the John Birch Society, and Stop ERA were asked to write and personally contact their local legislators, there was no systematic lobbying program. A spokesperson for Stop ERA confessed that she didn't know how many such contacts were made or letters sent. "I contacted some legislators at the Capitol, but there wasn't time to contact all," she added.

It was fairly typical of opposition strategy that one individual attempt to influence all legislators. For example, a state leader of the American Party spent $60 on a 14-page letter to all members of the state house of representatives. A leader of HOW went to the capitol each morning for the first two weeks of the 1974 session to distribute a set of 14 cartoons opposing the ERA.[31]

Georgia opponents were perhaps most effective in linking opposition to the ERA with deeply rooted social values. Although all the customary objections to the ERA were reportedly reiterated by Georgia opponents in their appeals to legislators, two points in particular were emphasized which predictably would sway a southern legislature:

My primary objection to ERA is that it's a broad, general amendment which is open to interpretation. I think only an absolute fool would give an open amendment to the Supreme Court in light of what the Court has done in the last twenty-five years.

The ERA is a power grab by Washington. States' rights pertaining to women will go to the national government. We've already given up power to the feds in other Constitutional amendments. Why give up more power?

Illinois   The movement to obtain ERA ratification in Illinois combined many of the conventional methods of the Georgia Statewide Coalition with the more aggressive tactics of the new feminist groups in Georgia and G-ERA. ERA Central concentrated on gaining the cooperation of the house and senate leadership and, when the amendment was bottled up in committee, shifted its attention there. Through letters and personal visits, all Illinois legislators evidently heard from pro-ERA constituents.

ERA Central in 1974 appointed district coordinators in each of the 59 legislative districts. Even the opposition granted that the proponents' organization was strong and exerted greater political pressure. Referring to the difficulties she had encountered in motivating opponents, one group leader complained: "It's much harder to get a response from the average housewife than from these career girls who are being paid full-time to drum up the mail. We don't have that organization."

The pro-ERA lobbyists in Springfield scrupulously cooperated with each other and communicated their findings to their state headquarters, which had WATS lines for reaching their members. When an important vote on the ERA came up, members around the state could use a state-provided toll-free number, available to all citizens, to "dial-a-legislator" in the capital. The Springfield lobbyists also took weekly or biweekly headcounts, based largely on positions taken in the party caucuses, which were followed up by personal contacts from someone likely to be influential with the legislator.

ERA Central conducted its own headcounts via phone calls and questionnaires. Comments from legislators concerning the reasons underlying their opposition to the amendment proved helpful and highly illuminating. One respondent, for example, apparently felt no concern over his opposition even though he believed "equal rights are God-given and that people who discriminate against women will be punished in *heaven*." Other remarks indicated the extent to which issues such as the draft, protective labor legislation, abortion, and rape laws have been determining factors.

Advocates in this state, too, were forced to participate in a debate which had expanded far beyond the virtues and defects of the ERA itself. As in Georgia, some supporters wondered if their rational approach was the correct one. A female attorney observed:

> We haven't really spoken to the emotional issues as well as I feel we should. I proposed last year that we have a really hot-blooded person speak in favor of the ERA just as they have really emotional speakers in opposition. Schlafly gets up and pleads. We're so rational, so cool, so reasonable about it and I don't know that that works. I don't think we've dealt with why this is such a fear and how to reassure the legislature that this is a law we're changing, that it guarantees equality for people who have had trouble with equality and that it doesn't change how women relate to men and children. That, I think, is their major fear.

Phyllis Schlafly personally lobbied in Springfield in 1972, as did several other opponent leaders. Beginning in 1973, mass gatherings of opponents, primarily women with children, were held in Springfield. During the 1974 legislative session, between 20 and 40 opponents appeared in the capitol every Wednesday. They brought placards, distributed literature and baked goods, and spoke with legislators.

One supporter, however, contended that the opposition was not very active, and this could not be disconfirmed. Opponents in Illinois were unaware of any organized lobbying network in Springfield similar to that of proponents. Opposition group leaders were uncertain whether current legislative headcounts or merely previous ERA voting records were used to guide their campaign involving primarily mass mailings, letters, phone calls, petitions, and personal contacts with local legislators. But even here they faced deep frustrations in trying to activate their constituencies. According to two Illinois opponents:

> One of the biggest problems is to get women to do anything or write letters. Very few will even write letters. I've tried to get a letter-writing campaign going but it's very difficult. Maybe they *do* write letters but don't tell us. I went to Springfield last year but no one else from my group was able to go. They all had excuses—child care, one woman's husband refused to let her go, another was having a rug delivered.

> People like us have very limited time and it would be against our nature to go out and organize because our main job-priority is the fact of staying in the home. If we put that aside for five years or even five months, we're in effect doing just what we're fighting against. The vast majority of women are doing what comes naturally to women, being homemakers and being in the home and they're not political activists. . . . This is not something they're concerned with but when I say would you really want the things ERA will bring and I enumerate them, they say, "Heavens no, but nobody will pass that."

Like their counterparts in Georgia and Texas, opponents of the ERA in Illinois did not appear to fit the model of the effective interest group to the degree that proponents did, according to these criteria: level of activity and legislative interaction, constituent contacts, and contacts with legislative leaders and committee members. Conclusions concerning either side's use of societal values in making their appeals will be held in abeyance.

Disruptive Tactics, Electoral Threats, and Other Nontraditional Methods

Although in several respects, as noted above, proponents excelled in traditional interest group politics, many of the tactics and strategies used by proponents are often considered counterproductive. Disruptive tactics are often viewed as illegitimate by decision makers since they violate the political rules of the game. Even resort to an unusual, though not disruptive, stratagem may alienate the legislator, accustomed to more conventional methods of lobbying. The use of electoral sanctions—by threatening either to withhold campaign support or to actively recruit and support an opposing candidate—also may be resented by the legislator and may even deepen his/her resistance to the lobbyist's entreaties. Despite this, ERA proponents, as well as opponents, have at times appeared to be relatively unconstrained by existing political and community norms.

Perhaps certain of these tactics *are* traditional, but with a feminine twist. Instead of the fifth of liquor, passed from male lobbyist to male legislator with a modicum of discretion, legislators have found a different type of gift in their mailboxes and on their desks. Owing to the donors' close identification with the housewife role, homemade bread and other baked goods have been a favorite gift of opposition women in almost all late-ratifying and unratified states. In Tennessee, members of AWARE went onto the floor of the house of representatives to personally distribute their bread until they were removed for illegal lobbying.

Proponent women have also been willing to display their culinary abilities. On Valentine's Day, local League of Women Voters members in Florida sent cookies to their legislative delegations, accompanied by valentines reading, "Be Our Valentine." On the first anniversary of congressional passage, North Carolina NOW sent birthday cakes to all ERA supporters in the state legislature, and pacifiers to all the opponents, with a note saying, "NOW will not be pacified till the ERA is ratified."

Both sides have indulged in a bit of role reversal by sending flowers. Legislators in Arizona and Ohio received red carnations from amendment supporters; Indiana legislators got yellow and white daisies from opponents after the ERA was defeated.

The more disruptive tactics appear to fall into one of two categories: those bearing a close resemblance to the methods of the 1960s black civil rights movement and those more closely related to the "media events" of the new feminist movement. In the first grouping are such strategies as the mass rally at the state capitol and parades or marches, utilized by both sides. The "pray-ins" staged by members of Catholic Women for the ERA on the steps of state capitols in unratified states are highly derivative from the black civil rights movement, as are the all-night "vigils" that have been used on occasion by both sides.

The second type of disruptive maneuver brings to mind the infamous 1968 Miss America contest demonstration.[32] The ERA has inspired several similar examples of street theater and symbolic gestures by proponents. What is surprising is that many of these events have occurred in the traditionalistic Deep South, a region which ordinarily would be least receptive. One possible explanation is that where goal achievement is least likely, all that remains for supporters is symbolic action.

In South Carolina, the Bicentennial reenactment parade of the first state legislature was held on a street newly painted with a red, white, and blue "ERA Now!" message courtesy of NOW, members of which held up signs in the crowd reading, "No taxation without equal rights," "Betsy Ross could do more than sew," and "Finish the Revolution." Broward County, Florida NOW staged a carnival, complete with effigy piñatas of the anti-ERA legislators, a "Pin the Tail on the Male Chauvinist Pig" game, and a "kissing booth" for pro-ERA legislators only. After a particularly bitter committee defeat for the amendment in Virginia in 1974,[33] the northern Virginia chapter of NOW presented House Majority Leader (and committee chairperson) James Thomson with a red, white, and blue floral arrangement inside a child's potty, suitably inscribed, "To Watergate on the James—[State Attorney General] Miller and Thomson, Plumbers, Inc."

Even though some highly original offensive measures have been taken by those in the South, Georgia groups have rarely adopted them. Beyond presenting a token flower or loaf of homemade bread to legislators, Georgia women have generally refrained from the dramatic performance. Exceptions are G-ERA's annual parade and rally along Peachtree Street to the capitol and periodic demonstrations in the capitol by delegations of opposition women from all over the state. In the opinion of the Statewide Coalition, ERA support had already progressed beyond the stage of public demonstration.

This latter viewpoint was taken by ERA Central in Illinois at various times as well, although the coalition held a sit-in in 1974 in the mayor's office following a rally in front of the

Chicago Civic Center and supporters have come to Springfield *en masse* on several occasions, including a rally in 1976 which drew an estimated 12,000 people from more than 30 states. Supporters have been advised that such mass gatherings, replete with picket signs, only reinforce the association of ERA with radical women's liberationists for less urbane downstate legislators. But ERA opponents in Illinois have also orchestrated mass gatherings in the capitol. In 1973, baby girls were brought to the legislature wearing signs around their necks pleading, "Don't draft me!" A more typical dramatic expedient of opponents has been to deliver various types of homebaked goods to the legislature. Illinois proponents have countered with tearoses, forget-me-nots, and an eggs Benedict brunch prepared by Housewives for the ERA.

In an effort to disassociate the amendment from the women's liberation movement, proponents in some states tried to play down the participation of new feminist groups such as NOW and to place middle-aged members of BPW and the League in the most visible roles as hearings witnesses and coalition leaders. Ironically, the difficulties these latter women encountered in obtaining ERA ratification instilled in them a greater appreciation of feminism and even militancy. A coalition leader in Wyoming was warned by Governor Stanley Hathaway that militant tactics would spell defeat for the amendment. She nodded in agreement, but added, "Governor, I want you to know that in my heart I *feel* militant."[34] Even in Georgia, where national observers agree the greatest split over strategy has occurred, a leader of one of the new feminist groups noted that the legislative obstacles placed in the path of ERA "angered a great many women and made them more militant than I've ever been able to do and I've been working at it." Or, as another young feminist leader put it:

> These women this year began saying things like: "I'm as much of a feminist as you!" They didn't call themselves "feminists" last year. Another thing is that they keep using the words "in sisterhood." Fantastic! These women themselves have begun to be proud of the fact that they are considering themselves "feminists." When a little old 80-year-old woman says, "I'm as much of a feminist as you 25-year old women!" . . . then you

know that feminism is beginning to seep into people's minds and it's really an exciting thing.

This recent sense of militancy among the more traditional proponent groups may also account for the adoption in many unratified states of a strategy based on a tough philosophy of "Don't bother to change their minds, just change their votes." Although most interest groups try to communicate power without going to the trouble and expense of actually defeating someone at the polls, the women's groups in this case were not risking a reputation for political clout because they had no such reputation. Rather, they could only benefit from *any* electoral successes.

At the June 1974 convention of the National Women's Political Caucus, it was suggested that ERA proponents: (1) Find a prospective pro-ERA opponent for anti-ERA legislators, one who was willing to withdraw if the incumbent changed his/ her position on the amendment, and so inform the incumbent. (2) Identify ERA opponents whose reelection was in doubt and *loudly* campaign against them, thus intimidating others when they were defeated.

In 1974, in 9 unratified states, 30 incumbents opposed to the amendment were defeated by "pro" challengers, while only one "pro" incumbent was defeated by a challenger opposed to the ERA.[35] Douglas Bailey of Bailey, Deardourff, and Eyre observed that these defeats provided:

> clear evidence of the power of women's groups to target legis-
> lators who opposed the issue. It was not just the switch of some
> "anti" to "pro" votes. It was the implied threat that this could
> happen to anyone. I think an awful lot of people who opposed
> ERA in the past will have to rethink their position this year.[36]

Electoral threats, though risky, have apparently proven viable for proponents.

Texas   Since Texas ratified the ERA in 1972 with only nine dissenting votes in the house and by voice vote in the Senate, there was no organized move for electoral retribution in the November 1972 election. One opponent, however, noted that his "no" vote *was* used against him in his next two candidacies, the second of which he lost.

Georgia   In Georgia, the legislature had already adjourned in 1972 before the ERA was submitted to the states for ratification. However, the Georgia Commission on the Status of Women, in cooperation with the League and BPW, contacted all 1972 legislative candidates and requested that they sign written pledges to support the amendment in 1973. Pledges were received from 91 successful house candidates, a comfortable majority. Many, however, reneged on their pledges in early 1973, protesting that they didn't know what they were signing.[37]

Opponents in Georgia related that they did not use electoral threats. Leaders of the Statewide Coalition were divided on whether or not their groups had done so. The conflicting reports seemed to result from differing interpretations of what constitutes an electoral threat. For example, one spokesperson denied using electoral threats, but readily admitted that she had said she would not campaign for anyone who voted against the ERA. The Statewide Coalition by and large pursued a passive-aggressive approach to electoral threats, using arguments such as:

> "You realize that your most active campaign supporters and workers are those groups for ERA, so if we don't get satisfaction from you, you've lost your staff, so you need to think about this." This was used with friends in the legislature or those who knew us well enough that they weren't going to turn around and say, "Don't push me against the wall." For the most part this message was conveyed by our friends in the legislature who would say, "Do you realize what they could do to you? They could actually run a candidate against you."

Illinois   In Illinois, where the amendment was twice defeated in the house of representatives in 1972, a campaign against several of those who voted against it was waged in the November elections. ERA supporters lacked sufficient organization at that juncture to be effective, however, and this may have reduced their credibility with legislators when electoral threats were made later. One vocal opponent spoke gleefully of his 2 to 1 victory in 1972 despite the antagonism of ERA proponents. Another anti-ERA legislator told ERA supporters, "Well, I was up for election in 1972 and no one defeated me on it, so why should I be afraid of it now [in 1974]?"

In 1974, supporters in Illinois followed a more complex electoral strategy. Instead of relying solely on targeting opposition legislators for defeat, they decided to also work *for* ERA supporters and to exploit disillusion with the Watergate-tainted Republican Party to the advantage of the ERA. Republican legislators were told, "The Republican Party is in enough trouble. Get behind it. It's going to happen anyway."

Amendment proponents expressed satisfaction with the outcome of the 1974 state elections. Two prominent anti-ERA legislators lost in the primaries, and others in the general election. Especially sweet was the defeat of the incumbent from Phyllis Schlafly's hometown of Alton. In 1975–76, the representative from Ms. Schlafly's legislative district supported the ERA. Of the five senators targeted by Chicago NOW, one was defeated in November and three others came to support the amendment before their re-election.

As in Georgia, all opposition group leaders denied using electoral threats. However, several felt such intimidation by proponents had been effective and expressed a willingness to use similar tactics in the future. One legislative supporter from the Chicago area did note that during the 1974 primary campaign a "Committee to Identify Legislators Who Want to Draft Your Daughter" had placed classified ads in the district newspapers of pro-ERA legislators denouncing that representative's position on the amendment.

Legislative Responses to the Lobbying Campaigns

Lobbying by both sides had reached such a fever pitch by 1973 that several weeks before the floor votes, many state legislators began to decline to discuss the ERA with lobbyists on either side. As legislators became entrenched in their positions, opinion either pro or con, but particularly that running counter to their own, served as an irritant. Although one study found a low awareness of lobbying activity in general among legislators,[38] virtually every one in the unratified and late-ratifying states was cognizant of the phenomenon.

This was certainly true of legislators in Georgia and Illinois. As a rule, they confirmed that proponents were far better organized. Contacts with established proponent groups were somewhat more frequently remembered as well. However, any implications of greater perceived legitimacy for these were offset by several other factors. Legislators reported that most contacts came from those outside their districts. Furthermore, they felt that the general public was as uninterested in the ERA as they themselves were. Any tactical differences between the two sides were blurred. In this case, *what* was said and *how* it was said was less important to legislators than the fact that they were trapped in the middle of a tremendous conflict between two active forces.

Texas   Although there *was* only limited lobbying for the ERA in Texas during the special session, several legislators—interviewed almost two years after Texas ratification—could recall no contacts from groups. "Very little public interest was generated," stated one ERA sponsor. Others remembered hearing from BPW and the League of Women Voters through phone calls, petitions, and personal letters. One legislator, who voted against the amendment, did report some interest in his district in the form of an anti-ERA petition listing between 600 and 700 names. Another opponent reported receiving mail from all over the state, saying in effect:

> "Let those busybody, 'do-gooders' who don't know whether they're men or women, let them go to blazes. Leave us alone. We like it the way it is." They weren't group members, just private individuals who didn't relate to Gloria Steinem, Mrs. Asbug [*sic*], or any other of those women's lib movements.

Perhaps the nine legislators in Texas who voted against the amendment in 1972 did receive letters and other expressions of opposition opinion. The majority of legislators, however, did not recall any great "hue and cry" over the amendment from any group or individual. Most reported that anti-ERA mail (principally from Arizona and other states) arrived in Texas after ratification, indicating that the potential may have existed for conflict on the scale of Georgia or Illinois.

Georgia   There was no lack of awareness of the groups on each side of the ERA controversy in Georgia. The League, BPW, and NOW were most readily identified as supporters, although several legislative opponents also mentioned the

Socialist Workers Party and the Atlanta Lesbian Feminist Alliance as examples of proponent groups. The John Birch Society and the DAR were the most frequently cited groups in opposition. "Stop ERA" was perceived as a slogan rather than as an organized group by legislators, who recalled Stop ERA's placards blanketing the capitol in 1973. The ERA campaign was viewed as primarily an organized group effort on the part of proponents. Opponents did not appear to be as well-organized, according to legislators, but, it was agreed, they still turned out in large numbers. "The public" as individuals were not felt to be concerned about the amendment.

All legislators reported receiving a large volume of mail on the ERA as well as phone calls, personal visits, and petitions. One supporter observed that most stereotyped mail was received from opponents. Another legislator remarked of both sides:

> A lot of the mail was organized and not very effective since it used the same wording. As with most groups that are amateur lobbyists, they made a mistake in directing their efforts just at the study committee and not at their own representatives. Mail from one area [Atlanta] which is unrepresentative of the state is disregarded.

Despite the central role that district contacts played in the self-described strategies of both sides, several legislators reported few or no contacts on the ERA from her/his constituents. One representative, who was on the ERA study committee, had never received any question on the amendment when appearing at public functions in his district; he estimated that he had received only 10 personal contacts from constituents. Another legislator estimated that 60–70 percent of his mail and personal contacts came from outside his district.

Although one legislator felt opponents were more aggressive and intimidating than were proponents, most legislators—regardless of their own stance—seemed to object equally to some of the approaches of both sides:

> It got to the point where legislators were becoming irritated by the militancy of both sides. Some of the most militant people I've ever seen were for it and against it . . . abusive letters and language. . . . Proponents and opponents couldn't even consider

having another side since the issue became so emotional. . . . No one likes to be pressured into anything. (A supporter)

Some women were courteous. Some cried. Some were extremely rude. Some threatened. Most were pleasant on both sides. Most weren't open-minded. (An opponent)

Some proponents took the position that if a legislator agreed with them, he was brilliant. If he disagreed, he was stupid. That is an unfortunate approach to take because many legislators in good faith had reservations about the ERA. (A supporter)

Both sides had signs but only proponents had full-scale demonstrations. The opponents just stood in the halls. Everywhere you'd go there would be a woman you'd have to weed your way through. They'd grab you by the arm and want to talk to you. . . . Some women tried to use their feminine touch to get to legislators. They'd put their arms around you and this irritated the men. Some demanded that legislators support the ERA and didn't leave them any leeway. The opponents tried to show why ERA was wrong. One woman told me, "I don't want to be liberated. I want my husband to fall at my feet and worship me." (An opponent)

All this activity was doubly annoying because, as one legislator confided, her colleagues really were not interested in the ERA: "They just wished they could have the cup pass."

Illinois Legislators in Illinois recalled communications from a broad range of groups on both sides including ad hoc groups such as Stop ERA and Right to Be a Woman and the pro-ERA coalition, ERA Central. Significantly, established groups such as the National Council of Catholic Women and the Illinois Federation of Republican Women's Clubs—both likely to be important to certain legislators—were identified with the opposition. But the League of Women Voters was termed the most respected and thus most effective group on the ERA by one of the leading legislative opponents.

According to one legislative sponsor, proponents really did not become well-organized until 1974. And the general feeling in the legislature was that opponents never became well-organized:

The opposition has not been effective. That's been one of the greatest problems that those opposing ERA are faced with. They do not have the effective lobby that the proponents have. It seems the squeaky wheel gets the grease. (An opponent)

The proponents are extremely active and are rather militant in their demands that either we support ERA or our political careers are going aglimmering. The opposition is also active and vocal but less organized. It seems to be organized more on an ad hoc basis. You get little letters from here and there. . . . Stop ERA is the biggest anti-organization and, I daresay, that's Mrs. Schlafly and about three of her friends in Alton. (An opponent)

The opposition groups are less organized but they began later. Also this is a swell coming from women who are not necessarily members of an organized group and that's the kind of women who are in my district. (An opponent)

It was clear, however, that Ms. Schlafly herself wielded much personal influence in her home-state legislature. Legislative opponents described her as "very knowledgeable," "well-informed," and "very much a lady." And legislators reportedly found Stop ERA's gifts of food and flowers amusing:

They don't buy anyone's vote but they aren't designed to do that—just to call attention to the fact that the proponents consider housewives a slave and a servant. (An opponent)

Legislators reported receiving letters, phone calls, and visits on weekends. One opponent, however, observed that the bulk of pro-ERA mail came from Chicago, which is outside her district. Another, a proponent, complained that headcounts were taken too frequently by amendment supporters. There was also general agreement among the legislators that women on both sides had much to learn about approaching a legislator on an issue of public policy:

They think all we need is to be pressured, but that's when we look the other way. The grabbing, pushing, "you gotta," the valentines that say, "Roses are red, violets are blue, vote for ERA or we're in for you," don't do any good. They're very unprofessional lobbyists, very extreme on both sides. Both say things that aren't so. (An opponent)

The supporters really do their cause a disservice in their tactics. The more aggressive proponents create an image of the liberated aggressive woman which is not popular with opponents, especially since the opposition argument is the breakdown of the family unit. (A supporter)

One legislator dismissed the ERA as an issue about which at least 80 percent of Illinois was unconcerned. According to an opponent, "The average person doesn't know what ERA is. To men it means Earned Run Average. To women, it's equal pay." Nor were the predominantly male legislators really interested in it, since it was not perceived as directly affecting them or their districts. Instead, it was increasingly viewed as an issue which had already been considered in several sessions and was now taking time which should be devoted to other matters of greater importance to them. However, spokespersons for both sides in the legislature believed (incorrectly thus far) that this legislative fatigue would facilitate eventual ratification.

> The legislators are interested in it but sick of it too. We've already gone through it once this year [1974] but somehow the proponents are able to produce Easter again and it's rising again from the dead to haunt us. I detect a note of weariness and a willingness to vote for it just to get it off our respective backs. I don't think it's a burning issue in the legislature with anyone except the women who've made it almost their sole cause. (An opponent)

> At first legislators were amused by amateur ERA lobbyists, didn't realize this was a serious issue. Then secondly they began to be a little edgy, irritated, and uncomfortable. Now I think it's mixed. They are tired of answering the mail on it. I think there's a tendency now just to wish it would go away. And this could work in our favor. If you want that tooth to stop aching, you might just as well pull it out and go on to other things. . . . I think they've gotten to the point that they want it to pass, whether or not they vote for it, because that's the only way it will go away. (A supporter)

Summary and Conclusions

The nature of the campaigns waged in the states by proponents and opponents of the ERA suggests some possible explanations for why it has not yet been ratified by the requisite number of state legislatures. Both models of conflict provide useful insights into these nonratifications.

If the lobbying campaigns are viewed solely as a conflict between competing interest groups, proponents had an advantage over opponents of the ERA in the formulation and implementation of traditional lobbying strategies. They were familiar with the basic principles of effective lobbying. Opponents, conversely, rarely articulated definitive and complex strategies for influencing legislators. Nor, it was generally agreed, did the opposition match their adversaries in sheer organization. Opponents probably relied too heavily on the use of mail and petitions, neglecting personal contacts with legislators by constituents in the districts and a formal lobbying network in the capitol. It was the change-oriented group which tended to be more active than the group attempting to preserve the status quo. Proponents, unlike opponents, also effectively used an electoral strategy in later phases of their campaign, albeit at the cost of causing resentment among some legislators.

The supporters' lobbying efforts were nonetheless flawed in ways that would predictably impair their chances of success. In Georgia, and to a lesser extent in Illinois, lobbying strategies were not fully operational in many areas of the state. Several legislators either were not contacted or were contacted by those outside their districts. There may also have been excessive attention directed toward getting the amendment out of committee, leaving too little time to build support for the ERA in the floor votes.

Legislators were also highly critical of the approaches used by both sides in their personal contacts. Despite the emphasis placed upon "ladylike" and low-keyed behavior in their strategy, the supporters nonetheless were perceived as "militant" by legislators. As females, both sides received a courteous hearing in the initial stages of the conflict, which may have worked in favor of the more active proponents. However, many of the nontraditional and disruptive tactics adopted, coupled with the fact that female lobbyists are still a novelty in many state legislatures, caused a surreal or circuslike atmosphere to surround the ERA campaign. As the conflict heightened, access was more frequently denied.

An additional problem faced by proponents was that, despite a coalition composed of well-known and well-established organizations, they were *not* perceived by legislators as more legitimate petitioners than opponents. Even in the face of national polls showing majority opinion in favor of the ERA and the heavy lobbying campaigns waged by both sides, legislators felt "the public" was not interested or involved in the issue. Furthermore, the ERA and its supporters were linked with the women's liberation movement, an association which was extremely detrimental to proponent efforts to influence conservative male legislators.

On the other hand, the close association of opposition leaders with ultraconservative political organizations was rarely denounced or perhaps even recognized by legislators and thus did not reduce the "legitimacy" of amendment opponents. At least in Georgia there was greater tolerance of the John Birch Society than of the new feminist movement.

Legislators correctly noticed that many women who had not previously been active in politics, either as individuals or as members of interest groups, had been drawn into the opposition ranks. The participation of these political amateurs over-shadowed that of their right-wing leaders in the eyes of legislators. Furthermore, many legislators perceived the opposition as composed of individuals, not as members of groups. This would be advantageous in a legislative system (typical of the South) labeling all interest groups "illegitimate." Finally, the opposition's weaker formal organization may not have been a liability in that there was a paternalistic attitude among some legislators toward those women who were conforming to a weaker political role.

The opposition was also able to use the traditional interest group technique of political letter writing very effectively to delay action on the ERA and then sometimes to defeat the resolution. By launching a vigorous mail campaign, opponents forced supporters to do likewise, thus diffusing the backlash which often comes from legislators who are irritated at having to use staff time to answer volumes of organized mail. Since mail was coming from both sides, the issue of the ERA itself became the target of legislative displeasure; overlooked was the fact that much of the opposition mail was of dubious origin.

These weaknesses of the proponents (and strengths of the opponents), as viewed from the perspective of traditional interest group politics, may be sufficient to explain the non-ratification of the ERA in certain states. However, the fact that the ERA became a matter of community conflict is essential to a full understanding of the dynamics of nonratification. In many instances, the above weaknesses and strengths resulted from the conversion of the ERA controversy into a community conflict. Proponents were unable to adhere to the political rules of the game. Instead, they were forced to adopt some of the methods of the group engaged in a community conflict.

Amendment opponents were very successful in attracting many members of the community, who ordinarily would not be involved in a political movement. They were also able to greatly expand the controversy to include topics only tangentially related to the amendment or, in some cases, completely unrelated. By the inclusion of topics on which the community was already divided, the level of controversy was heightened and the number of community participants greatly increased.

Not only was the debate over the ERA converted into a bitter ideological fight, but it also took on religious overtones. Proponents, with their essentially optimistic view of mankind, were slow to recognize the limitations of public education as an element of their general legislative campaign. If the opinion polls on the ERA are correct, there was actually no need for proponents to attempt a public education campaign as majority support already existed.

To supporters among the public at large, the need for the amendment may have seemed so apparent that they ignored appeals to contact legislators in its behalf. For those in opposition or undecided, the proponents' complex and legalistic interpretation of the amendment's potential impact only seemed to increase their confusion and fears.

Proponents were also handicapped in their public education campaign and in their attempts to establish and maintain contacts with legislators by the fact of the social values and symbols they could invoke to legitimize their goals. Opponents associated themselves with such valued institutions as the home, family, motherhood, and religion, as well as with the strong national traditions of anticommunism and all-male combat forces. Proponent groups, many of whom were already associated with the "public interest," had to rely on important but abstract values such as "equality" and "justice under the law."

Proponents were not advantaged by their greater reliance on a rational approach to the issue's merits, while opponents redefined, simplified, and distorted the original issues surrounding the ERA. Even though supporters had begun to realize that rationality often is not an asset, they *were* more restrained in stating their case for the amendment, particularly since proponents relied to a greater extent on face-to-face (rather than mail and phone) contacts. Yet, the level of conflict was so high that legislators failed to differentiate between the two sides, labeling both "emotional" and "irrational."

The statewide media, frequently sympathetic to the amendment but unwilling to forego a colorful story, played an important, if not central, role in the expansion of conflict by treating the anti-ERA arguments seriously and usually without editorial comment. Although the more skillful use of the media by proponents and the editorial endorsements by major urban newspapers may have influenced some legislators, the main impact of the media was probably to increase public awareness and to give credence to opposition views.

In states like Georgia and Illinois where the ERA became a full-scale community conflict, that model of conflict provides the more cogent explanation of lobbying strategies and their legislative perceptions. Even though attempts were made by proponents to lower the level of controversy and even avoid it, and to conduct a lobbying compaign in accordance with traditional interest group tactics, such efforts failed. Only in states like Texas, where the legislature perceived little or no conflict, was the issue resolved by traditional interest group politics.

NOTES

1. See Wayne L. Francis, *Legislative Issues in the Fifty States: A Comparative Analysis* (Chicago: Rand McNally, 1967), pp. 11–14.
2. The words "Equal Rights Amendment" have apparently become a red flag. A sizable segment of the population agrees that equality of rights under the law should not be denied or abridged because of sex but are opposed to "the ERA."

3. U.S., Congress, Senate, 8 February 1972, *Congressional Record* 118: 3072–73. This poll originally appeared in the Sunday supplement *Parade*, 26 September 1971.

4. *John Birch Society Bulletin*, February 1974, p. 24.

5. See an editorial in the *National Observer*, 1 March 1975, for an analysis of the reaction by ERA opponents to the endorsement of the ERA by First Lady Betty Ford. According to Mary Leonard, author of the editorial, Ms. Ford as faithful wife and devoted mother is the very model of the woman opponents believe should be repulsed and threatened by the ERA. "They feel pretty secure and smug when they can label the ERA as the offspring of radical feminism. Their ground isn't quite so solid when women much like themselves . . . start talking about equality and justice."

6. Jaquie Davison, *I Am a Housewife* (New York: Guild, 1972), pp. 68–69.

7. "The Precious Rights ERA Will Take Away from Wives," *Phyllis Schlafly Report* 7 (August 1973): 1.

8. John I. Schmitz, "Look Out! They're Planning to Draft Your Daughter," *American Opinion* 15 (November 1972): 3.

9. "Should Women Be Drafted?" *Phyllis Schlafly Report* 6 (March 1973): 2.

10. Schmitz, p. 6.

11. "What's Wrong with 'Equal Rights' for Women?" *Phyllis Schlafly Report* 5 (February 1972): 3.

12. Ibid.

13. "Are You Financing Women's Lib?" *Phyllis Schlafly Report* 7 (February 1974): 3.

14. In her February 1975 *Report*, Ms. Schlafly claims that forces in our society which have sought to weaken the local police in recent years through civilian review boards have now switched their tactic to one of placing women on the force. The ERA, as it applies to sex discrimination in employment, thus is viewed as a tool to destroy the local police.

15. Quoted in Lisa Cronin Wohl, "White Gloves and Combat Boots: The Fight for ERA," *Civil Liberties Review* 1 (Fall 1974): 80.

16. Rev. Bob Spencer, "Equal Rights for Women," in his *God's Truth for Today* (Atlanta, 1973), p. 56.

17. Quoted in the *South Bend Tribune*, 15 February 1973.

18. V. O. Key, Jr., *Politics, Parties, and Pressure Groups*, 5th ed. (New York: Crowell, 1964), p. 103.

    A blatantly sexist statement is found in Graham Wootten, *Interest-Groups* (Englewood Cliffs, N.J.: Prentice-Hall, 1970), p. 42. "But in [the legislator's] eyes most women's organizations probably appear as women themselves appear—of aesthetic appeal rather than political import."

19. Although many men have appeared as witnesses at legislative hearings, lobbying has been done primarily by women. Thus the amendment has been associated solely with equal rights for women. One

conclusion of the report on the ERA received from Bailey, Deardourff, and Eyre was that the involvement of men in lobbying and through men for ERA groups could be a valuable approach. Male involvement could impress upon legislators that this is not just a woman's issue, that this is a serious issue that cannot easily be dismissed.

20. For other recent studies of the role of women in the formation of public policy, see Jo Freeman, *The Politics of Women's Liberation* (New York: Longman, 1975), Anne N. Costain, "A Social Movement Lobbies: Women's Liberation and Pressure Politics," paper presented at the Annual Meeting of the Southern Political Science Association, 1975, and Kathleen McCourt, *Working-Class Women and Grass-Roots Politics* (Bloomington, Ind.: University of Indiana Press, 1977).

21. Raymond A. Bauer et al., *American Business and Public Policy* (New York: Atherton, 1963), p. 393.

22. Quoted in Martin Gruberg, *Women in American Politics: An Assessment and Sourcebook* (Oshkosh, Wis.: Academic, 1968), p. 87.

23. Harmon Zeigler and Michael A. Baer, "The Recruitment of Lobbyists and Legislators," *Midwest Journal of Political Science* 12 (November 1968): 493–513.

24. Bauer et al., pp. 388–95. Frank Bonilla, "When Is Petition 'Pressure'?" *Public Opinion Quarterly* 20 (Spring 1956): 39–48.

25. To the extent that a sharing of political power exists between the sexes, problems touching upon the home and the community are assigned to women. A woman lobbying on such issues might be adjudged a more "legitimate" petitioner because of her sex. For a discussion of the sexual division of political labor, see James G. March, "Husband-Wife Interaction over Political Issues," *Public Opinion Quarterly* 17 (Winter 1953–54): 461–70; and Gabriel Almond and Sidney Verba, *The Civic Culture* (Boston: Little, Brown, 1965), pp. 329–32.

26. Quoted in Claire Safran, "What You Should Know about the Equal Rights Amendment," *Redbook* 141 (June 1973): 62ff.

27. Quoted in Safran.

28. Quoted in Wohl, p. 86.

29. Eileen Shanahan, "Stiff Fight Looms over Ratification of Equal Rights Amendment," *New York Times*, 29 January 1974, p. 15.

30. See Leila Sussman, "Mass Political Letter Writing in America: The Growth of an Institution," *Public Opinion Quarterly* 23 (Summer 1959): 205–12.

31. The cartoons portray an America (presumably after ERA ratification) where men must take pregnancy tests, women are beasts of burden, children are reduced to robots by federal day-care centers, and men and women fight (and urinate) side-by-side.

32. On Saturday, September 7, 1968, radical feminists from three states and Washington, D.C., demonstrated in Atlantic City, New Jersey, site of the pageant. A live sheep was crowned Miss America, and a trashcan served as a receptacle for items symbolic of traditional feminin-

ity: bras, girdles, high-heeled shoes, and haircurlers. No bras were in fact burned.

33. During the February 27, 1974, meeting of the House Privileges and Elections Committee, a memorandum drafted by Virginia Attorney General Andrew Miller's office was read behind closed doors to committee members immediately preceding a final vote on the ERA resolution. The then secret interoffice memo suggested that the ERA would render illegal the use of separate male and female bath and toilet facilities in public buildings and institutions. See Nancy D. Joyner, "The Commonwealth's Approach to the Equal Rights Amendment," *University of Virginia Newsletter* 50 (15 May 1974): 35.

34. Quoted in Safran.

35. The League of Women Voters, *ERA Yes!* November 1974, p. 1. In November 1976, 14 anti-ERA legislators were defeated; no figures are available on primary losses suffered by ERA opponents.

36. Quoted in Isabelle Shelton, "Five More States Needed to Ratify ERA This Year," *Philadelphia Evening Bulletin*, 9 January 1975.

37. Women in Oklahoma and Arizona complained in 1975 that legislators who had run on a pro-ERA platform and had signed pledges in support of the amendment were voting against the ERA. In the Arizona senate the ERA lost by two votes in 1975. In the Oklahoma house, the ERA lost by six votes, defeated by nine reneging representatives. This reportedly happened again in 1977 in other states.

38. Oliver Garceau and Corinne Silverman, "A Pressure Group and the Pressured: A Case Report," *American Political Science Review* 48 (September 1954): 672–91.

5 Legislative Decision Making

Legislative responses to the ERA in the unratified states have ranged from rejection by a narrow majority in a floor vote to deliberate inaction in committee. It is these responses of legislatures in the unratified states which are of primary interest here because they illustrate the impact of interest group and community conflicts upon the decision process. But the responses of many of the ratified states are also significant in that they show how the decision process operates in the absence of conflict.

In 1972 and early 1973 numerous state legislatures suspended their rules in order to act with dispatch upon the resolutions to ratify the Equal Rights Amendment. In Hawaii, within 20 minutes after an employee of the state's legislative reference bureau heard of Senate passage from a secretary in Senator Daniel Inouye's Washington office, the president of the state senate presented a resolution to ratify. Within five minutes the state senate-passed resolution was before Hawaii house, and ratification (unanimous in both houses) was complete, making Hawaii the first state to ratify the ERA.

In five other states the amendment was ratified within two days of congressional submission. In Delaware, the state BPW president had recruited a sponsor for the amendment on March 7, 1972. A resolution to ratify was drafted by March 21, and on March 22 a representative of BPW called the Delaware sponsor from a phone outside the U.S. Senate gallery with news of Senate passage. By March 23, another unanimous ratification was achieved. A third such vote was also recorded that day in Nebraska, where the unicameral legislature voted to suspend customary rules and immediately took up the resolution on the floor, adopting it in a matter of minutes. And in New Hampshire also, at the urging of the governor, rules were suspended and the ERA was passed late in the day on March 23. Idaho, acting in joint session, ratified on March 24 with only nine dissenting votes. Iowa also ratified on the same date, during the last night of the legislative session.

Throughout 1972 and into the early months of 1973, state legislatures continued to act affirmatively upon the ERA.[1] Although after March 23 only West Virginia ratified it with no dissenting vote recorded, impressive margins continued to be summoned in its support. Rules were suspended in order to avoid referral to committee. Frequently no or only perfunctory hearings were held on the subject. Floor debate, too, was brief. Where group opposition to the ERA did arise, such activity reportedly had little effect.

In general, proponent groups had extraordinary control over the legislative process in 1972 and early 1973. They recruited sponsors for the ERA in several states. Supporters in Maryland worked with those legislators who were sponsoring separate ERA resolutions to get all but one to withdraw their resolutions so that quick ratification would be possible. The governor of Massachusetts consulted with proponent groups on their wishes concerning committee referral and open debate on the issue. (They requested neither.)

Powerful allies were active in the states as well. In Minnesota, the state's congressional delegation contacted the state's legislators in behalf of the amendment. Congresswoman Ella Grasso (D.-Conn.) called her state's legislators, and Congresswoman Margaret Heckler (R.-Mass.) met with Massachusetts proponents to discuss strategy. In Kentucky, U.S. Senator Marlowe Cook personally asked the governor to add ERA to the agenda of the 1972 special session, and the lieutenant governor of Kentucky worked with proponents on procedural matters. Even in those states where open hearings were held, it was not uncommon for only proponents of the amendment to appear as witnesses. And they were notably successful in 1972 in turning back opposition requests for the establishment of interim study committees; only in Connecticut and Vermont, where the lower houses defeated the ERA that year, were such committees established.

But at some point, most commonly in 1973, the proponents lost this control. The conditions surrounding ERA ratification campaigns evolved into those described in chapter 4; legislatures in unratified and late-ratifying states were subjected to heavy lobbying on both sides of the issue. The issue became so controversial that the legislature could not avoid holding open hearings on the subject. These often lasted all day or were held on several different days in various locations across the state, with live television coverage. Floor debates became prolonged and heated, with a large percentage of the legislators seeking the floor to "explain" their votes. With increasing frequency, legislators sought refuge in legislative procedure to delay or avoid entirely a public decision on the now controversial amendment.

The ERA in the Legislatures: The Formal Legislative Process

The responses of the legislatures in Texas, Georgia, and Illinois to the ERA span the range of kinds of decisions made on the amendment. Texas is typical of those states which quickly ratified it in the absence of conflict. Ratification was achieved in only three days from the date of introduction even though the resolutions were referred to committees in both houses and a public hearing was held in the house. Georgia is representative of states at the opposite end of the spectrum: those that have been able to delay or avoid definitive decision making on this issue of public controversy. The ERA was placed in a house study committee during the 1973 legislative session and by the end of the 1978 session, only one floor vote had been taken on the amendment in each house, both resounding defeats.

The responses of both state legislatures conform to those

suggested by the conflict models. Much interest group activity occurs in the absence of competition from other groups, and when this is the case decision makers will usually adopt the policy supported by groups active on a given issue. With the presence of conflict, however, the decision process is slowed. And if a community conflict is involved, there will be an attempt to avoid any definitive decision making. At a minimum, any decision is unlikely to result in the adoption of a new policy.

Illinois is typical of those states where the ERA has been a controversial issue for several legislative sessions. In some of these states, ratification has eventually been achieved after at least one defeat in committee or on the floor. In others, as in Illinois, ratification has not yet occurred. But in all, decision making on the issue has rarely been avoided. In Illinois, by June 1978, twelve floor votes on the ERA had been recorded, seven in the house and five in the senate, and several more had been taken on procedural matters directly related to the amendment's passage. The conflict may have prevented adoption of this new policy in Illinois, but support for the ERA apparently ran too strong to allow decision makers to withdraw from the conflict.

ERA Sponsors

The choice of a legislative sponsor for the ERA has proven to be an important factor in its support in the legislature. Both models of conflict stress the importance of elite support in influencing decision makers. And in the case of a community conflict, an active legislative sponsor is crucial in order to legitimize the policy.

The ideal of an active and effective sponsor has not always been met in the case of the ERA. Frequently, female legislators have served as the ERA's sponsors, a role which many report introduced a strain into their otherwise excellent relations with male colleagues.[2] Male legislators resented their female colleagues' sponsorship of a "women's issue." In states where male legislators have served as sponsors, they, too, have presented problems. Even when the sponsor is a powerful committee chairman or the majority leader, ratification is still not assured. A legislative leader, encountering public conflict over the ERA, has, in some states, withdrawn from a position of full and active sponsorship in order to conserve that leadership power. Unlike established groups and leaders outside the legislature, some legislative elites do appear to have withdrawn from or been neutralized by the statewide conflict over the amendment.

Proponent groups that were able to play a role in the selection of sponsors frequently faced a dilemma: whether to choose an enthusiastic, active, and cooperative female sponsor who lacked influence or a more influential but less cooperative male sponsor.

Texas   The sponsors of the original state house and senate resolutions to ratify the ERA in Texas had been the sponsors of the state ELRA. But an *opponent* of the state ELRA was the sponsor of the resolution that actually passed the Texas house of representatives. With an eye to his attempt to win election to the state senate in 1972, he recalled that in his past two election campaigns for the state house, the local BPW club had worked against him because of his opposition to the ELRA:[3]

> I was quite anxious, when this issue came along, to show them I was not prejudiced. . . . I talked to the Senate leadership, the people who authored the bill [in the Senate], and they [the senators] asked me to carry it in the House and I did. Of course, one of them and____ [the original House sponsor] were in a race for the Senate against each other and I'm sure that would have something to do with it.

Although women and women's groups were not active in recruiting the sponsors or in working with them for ratification, women indirectly played a crucial role. In order to gain the support (or at least avoid the opposition) of women in his race for the senate, a house sponsor was readily available. The sponsor in the senate was widely regarded as one of its most powerful members. Although the house sponsor was not recognized as particularly powerful, neither did he have any apparent liabilities. Both were considered effective sponsors.

Illinois   In Illinois, the ERA retained its three original female sponsors, from 1972 to 1975, although in 1974 a male senator was brought in as a second senate sponsor. The ERA then had a Republican sponsor and a Democratic sponsor in each house. Again, the amendment proponents outside the legislature played no role in their recruitment. Both the sponsors and proponent group leaders concede that there was no choice but to have these three women sponsor the amendment in 1972. "There were no other options; it was felt that this was the girls' baby," explained one leader.

The two female sponsors in the house reportedly were well-liked and one had close ties with her party's leadership. As for the senate sponsor, one group leader described her in these terms:

> [She] had union support and people owed her. She's been around long enough that she could put it together; she had enough savvy . . . but she's never been accepted. She's a regular the regulars could do without—but she wins, so they can't avoid her. I don't regard [her] as a problem.

Equally important, the original sponsors were willing to actively use their influence to win votes for the ERA among their colleagues. Nevertheless, they proved to have several political liabilities. Anti-Chicago sentiment runs high in downstate Illinois, an area where the ERA has encountered its strongest opposition. Yet all sponsors were from the Chicago area. In 1973, in response to an inquiry from ERA Central, several Republican house members stated that their votes on the ERA depended on who the sponsors were, a reference to a feeling that the women in the legislature were crossing party lines to share information and band together on women's issues. Supporters of organized labor in the legislature also recalled the move by female legislators, among them the ERA's sponsors, to permit meat sales to go on after 6:00 P.M., which was in effect a circumvention of the Meatcutter's Union contract. And most detrimental, the house sponsors played central roles in two partisan disputes in 1972 and 1973 (for an elaboration, see pp. 166–68). Despite their active support of the amendment, the sponsors in Illinois were handicapped in legitimizing the ERA by their sex and by their participation in these party skirmishes. In April 1975, the senate sponsor resigned her seat and recruited a male legislator as ERA sponsor. In 1977, in hopes of infusing new life into the amendment and attracting additional legislative support, a change was also made in house sponsorship. Four male legislators, including a Republican from Moline, assumed the role of main sponsors.

Georgia   In Georgia, proponents in 1972 had asked house majority leader (now governor) George Busbee to sponsor the ERA. They felt confident of ratification; Busbee had the power and the ability to pass the amendment. The majority leader, however, withdrew as sponsor two to three days before the legislature convened in 1973. As one supporting group leader described the situation:

> Busbee was committed for a year to sponsor the ERA. He was recruited by the Georgia Women's Political Caucus, the Commission on the Status of Women, and the Governor and he was most pleased to do it. He was planning to run for Governor and he thought it was a nice issue to tack on to get support from women's groups. In October–November 1972, the national controversy arose and he got out, but not in time for women's groups to recruit someone strong to get it through. He told us of the new sponsor after the fact.

As in other states, the coalescence of controversy effectively removed a capable sponsor from the arena of conflict.[4]

Proponent groups agreed that the new house sponsor was not an active or effective sponsor. Nor was he known as a particularly good legislator. Not only had he, by his own admission, not tried to build support for the amendment, but also he was unaware of *who* supported it in the house or who would be speaking for it during the floor debate. As one pro-ERA group leader disdainfully commented:

> He thought ERA only had 50 votes as of Sunday night. He thought he was dealing with a group of amateur women. He said, "You're not going to leave me out on the floor alone, are you?" We told him we had speakers all lined up.

Representative Busbee may not have been the only legislator to flee from the conflict, however. Although numerous cosponsors of a bill are the norm in the Georgia legislature, the ERA had none. According to the house sponsor, "most people I asked were not interested in cosponsoring it." Given the reluctance by Georgia house members to be overtly associated with the amendment, the legislator who served as sponsor may have been the best available choice because he was strategically placed, as chairperson of the committee to which the ERA was referred, to facilitate passage.

Legislative Leadership and Committee Action

Frequently in traditional interest group politics, an effective group will have already established working relationships with the chairpersons and members of committees which ordinarily consider legislation of concern to that group. In the case of the ERA, such a relationship rarely existed between legislators and groups on either side of the issue. Given the diverse committees to which the ERA was referred in the states (e.g., judiciary, human resources, executive), no generalizations can be made about the likelihood of committee members being either hostile or sympathetic to women's rights. The response of the leadership and committees to the amendment appeared to be based partially upon personal views on the issues involved but largely upon the dynamics of the conflict itself.

Texas   In Texas, the ERA had the support of the leaders in both houses, and committee consideration was both swift and favorable. Upon introduction in the senate on the first day (March 28, 1972) of the special session, the ERA was referred to the Committee on Transportation and was favorably reported back to the floor the next day.[5] The Transportation Committee, according to the senate sponsor, was the only one in the senate that had pending business; the other committees had not been organized for this three-day session, called to pass a new campaign finance law and highway legislation. In the house, the original house resolution and the senate-passed version were both referred on March 29 to the Committee on Constitutional Amendments. Both were reported back favorably the following day.

Georgia   When the amendment was being considered by the Georgia house of representatives, 1973–74, the house leadership, divided on the ERA, did not attempt to exert any influence whatsoever on the committee or other members of the legislature. In 1975–78, when the senate considered the amendment, the presiding officer, Lieutenant Governor Zell Miller, did take a strong position in support. This suggests that the legislative leadership was neutralized by the ERA controversy in its initial stages just as were prospective house sponsors.

Members of the Special Judiciary Committee, to which the ERA was referred in the house in 1973, were also reluctant to publicly support or oppose the amendment, even though the committee chairman was the amendment's sponsor. That year, ostensibly at the request of women's groups,[6] the ERA, by a vote of 11 to 3, had been put into a special subcommittee for further study, a common solution in Georgia for defusing controversial issues. The following year, in 1974, committee members, like their legislative leaders, retreated into neutrality, and the amendment was sent to the full house for a floor vote without a committee recommendation, a very unusual action in the Georgia legislative system.[7]

Illinois   Legislative leaders in Illinois, although divided on the ERA, were not neutralized, although proponents may have preferred this to the public opposition of several key leaders from 1973 on. Although the amendment encountered a somewhat less hostile committee response in Illinois than in Georgia, the committee system obstructed ratification to a degree which is exceptional in Illinois legislative politics. According to observers of Illinois government:

> Committee chairmen do not kill bills, do not delay bills, do not ignore bills, and rarely make a parliamentary ruling that will have an important effect on the future of a bill . . . the bill's sponsor requests that the chairman set a hearing on a particular date and every chairman will accede to such a request . . . committees tend to be unwilling to assume responsibility for formally killing a bill.[8]

Yet the ERA was defeated in committee in the senate in 1973 and again in 1975.

Although bills are often not referred to committee in the Illinois legislature,[9] it is unusual for a vote to remove a controversial bill from committee to receive the required majority. Such a bill is usually being held in committee because the legislature as a whole wishes to avoid a floor vote on the issue.

Yet a vote to discharge the ERA failed in 1973 by only two votes in the senate. And in 1974, rather than have the amendment referred to the Senate Executive Committee and certain burial, the sponsor asked that it not be sent to a committee. By a vote of 39 to 17, the senate acceded. Like their legislative leaders, Illinois legislators did not refuse to take public positions on the amendment.

The Hearings

Although the role of hearings in influencing legislative decision making is usually considered minimal, they do serve several functions. The more important the measure, the more likely it is that legislators have already reached a firm position and the voting pattern is predetermined and the hearing is designed to serve these other functions. Truman lists three:

> First, the hearing is a means of transmitting information, both technical and political, from various actual and potential interest groups to the committee. . . . A second use is as a propaganda channel through which a public may be extended and its segments partially consolidated or reinforced. A third function is to provide a quasi-ritualistic means of adjusting group conflicts and relieving disturbances through a safety valve.[10]

A fourth function, that of legitimation, is suggested by Freeman as particularly appropriate for new interest groups, especially those created by social movements. Attention from legislators through the hearings process and a public airing of their ideas help provide an aura of legitimacy for these new ideas and groups.[11]

All four functions have been served by the many public hearings on the ERA. The first—providing technical and political information—has been paramount for amendment proponents, eager to explain the beneficial impact of the ERA and to demonstrate their broad-based support. For the group engaged in traditional interest group politics, the most successful activities involve the distribution of information and research to legislators.

The third function—public hearing as safety valve—has undoubtedly been of greatest importance to legislators in states where debate over the amendment has reached a fever pitch. Where the issue has been considered in more than one session, little new information can be provided. Yet in several states public hearings have been scheduled annually. Because the ERA can only be ratified or not ratified (i.e., a compromise wording is not permitted), the losing side can be partially appeased by a "fair hearing" from decision makers. Proponents recognized the dangers inherent in open hearings, but conceded that once the ERA became the subject of public controversy, the legislature really had no choice but to schedule public hearings. Had the legislators attempted to lower the level of conflict by restricting public debate, they would have been vulnerable to charges of elitism and undemocratic tactics.

The primary danger inherent in open hearings from the perspective of proponents is the second function of legislative hearings: the expansion of conflict. As legitimate news, legislative hearings, more easily than other events, can capture the attention of the media. This function, and that of legitimation, have been of greatest importance to amendment opponents.

Texas   Although no hearing on the ERA was held in the Texas Senate Committee on Transportation, a hearing, regularly posted and open to the public, was held on March 30, 1972, in the House Committee on Constitutional Amendments. According to the minutes of that meeting, the "hearing" had only two witnesses, the sponsors of the two resolutions, and lasted from 9:55 to 10:20 A.M. As one sponsor recalled, he explained the need for and the potential impact of the amendment to the committee and a majority of the committee approved it without asking any questions of him. Public hearings on the ERA in Texas served none of the above mentioned functions; the house hearing was only ritualistic conformity to established legislative procedure. Proponents and opponents outside the legislature were unaware that such a hearing had been held.

Georgia   The Georgia house held two public hearings on the ERA in 1973. The first, in February, lasted five hours. About 40 witnesses, representing all the principal pro-ERA groups, testified in the amendment's favor. Another some 40 people, including Phyllis Schlafly, J. B. Stoner, and representatives of the Ku Klux Klan and the John Birch Society, testified against the ERA. A second hearing was held in September by the Special Study Subcommittee.

One member of the latter felt the hearings were beneficial, if only because of their pressure valve function:

> Such [hearings] allow people to get things off their chests and that helps those who attend [i.e., the witnesses], not those who are listening [i.e., the committee members]. They were a good thing because legislators let people know they were interested in their opinions but factual information and valuable data could have been gotten in one-fifth of the time in a closed hearing meeting.

Another member, less tolerant of the public hearing as propaganda instrument, agreed with his colleague that the witnesses conveyed no worthwhile information.

> The witnesses were very poor and were indoctrinated by their own organization's position papers. Few were lawyers. If we had it to do over, we would hold closed hearings. Both sides wanted to use the hearings to get before media, TV cameras, and the public to build up public support for their cause and position. The only satisfactory hearing is to have groups submit names of prospective witnesses with their backgrounds and let the legislators choose their witnesses. We didn't hear legal (i.e., lawyers) witnesses because the committee had to put up with a bunch of women raising hell. . . . They had two or three good speakers but most was a bunch of crap, on both sides really, just wild-eyed type things.

Both opponents and proponents were critical of the public hearings. The former felt the testimony was repetitive, particularly since the same people testified at both hearings. Members of the Statewide Coalition had hoped to avoid open hearings. As two proponent leaders explained:

> If you want to kill legislation, have open hearings. The ERA started going down that first weekend of the [1973] session, but the Feburary hearing just finished it.

> We worked long and hard not to have a public hearing. . . . They brought in Mrs. Schlafly. . . . We had considered doing this because we had national contacts, too, but we decided, no, that's

not cricket, we are Georgia women, the men will listen to us and of course we were just absolutely babes in the woods. . . . If it could have stayed a quiet, behind-the-scenes campaign, we would have passed it. . . . Schlafly was extremely effective. Legislators told us afterwards that we didn't win anything and we didn't lose anything. But she sat behind the speaker's stand with all the men who were running things. None of us were invited up there, not that we would have gone; it wasn't our place.

Proponents in Georgia were proud of their "well-organized, knowledgeable, reasonable, and dignified presentation" at the first hearing ("one of the best prepared public hearings in the history of the state"). Each witness was assigned a particular aspect of the ERA and time was carefully apportioned among the various group representatives. Opponents, on the other hand, were most pleased with their ability to outnumber proponents in the audience at the two hearings, thus giving the impression to reporters and the TV audience that theirs was the stronger side.

The February hearing did play a role in expanding the level of controversy over the ERA and for this reason was beneficial to opponents. Subsequently, both the committee and the sponsor attempted to contain the controversy by not scheduling further hearings, despite demands from some persons on both sides. After relenting, the Special Study Subcommittee was still able to restrict the conflict by deliberately giving short notice for the September hearing in order to reduce the number of those attending and giving testimony.[12]

Illinois   Several public hearings on the ERA have been held in Illinois, but none lasted beyond three hours. In 1972, proponent testimony was predominant in the first hearing in the Senate Executive Committee. The next year, realizing that committee members had already made up their minds, the chairperson restricted each side to 10 minutes. More recent hearings attracted an equal number of witnesses for each side and lasted from one to three hours.

From the viewpoint of the ERA's sponsors, the house held very fair hearings in 1973, but the senate counterpart was criticized. According to the sponsors:

> The House hearings were very satisfactory. One hour is long enough for each side, given the attention span of legislators. We were able to get all of our people on . . . a beautiful staging job . . . no repetition . . . outstanding people and organizations.

> The Senate had very unfair hearings. At the beginning [the chairperson] recognized Mrs. Schlafly and let the Senate sponsor make a brief statement but not present any of her witnesses so they all went home . . . a travesty of the legislative process.

Proponent group leaders echoed this criticism of the 1973 Senate Executive Committee hearings, but in general expressed satisfaction with their efforts to provide political and technical information. Topics were assigned and time allotted to each speaker, chosen for her or his anticipated political influence (based on partisan, regional, and interest group considerations).

Those in opposition to the amendment were highly critical of the way the various hearings were handled. Some had hoped to introduce a noted constitutional scholar from outside Illinois but were unable to learn the exact date of the hearing so that travel arrangements could be made. Another found that all house committee members had already taken a firm stand on the ERA; the 1973 hearings thus seemed to her a sham to give the public the impression that a study was being made.

But it was the 1972 senate hearing which most upset opposition leaders:

> In 1972, only proponents were heard in public hearings; opponents didn't know of the Senate hearing. In 1972, the Senate didn't care if people knew about ERA. They wanted a quick floor vote and they wanted it to pass.

The legislators appeared to have made a trade-off in their handling of public hearings. They were successful in holding down the level of conflict by imposing strict time limitations upon testimony and omitting full-scale hearings in each session. In so doing, the legislature chose to forego any possibly beneficial effects of the safety valve function. Opponents and proponents alike were frustrated by these time limitations and by frequent changes in scheduling. Proponents, however, seemed satisfied with their use of the hearings to convey information. Opponents seemed more concerned with a "fair hearing" than with using the forum for constituency-building and legitimation.

The Floor Debate   The prevailing view of floor debate is that speeches rarely influence many legislative votes. Their primary effect is to reinforce and activate views already held, and their purpose is to make a record for the individual legislator. The speech may be expected to pay off politically, whether with constituents, a lobbyist, the media, the governor, or a legislative colleague. Debate is also a means by which legislators can "explain" their vote and the intensity with which they hold that position in the event that this vote is or becomes the subject of controversy. Finally, floor debate can be used by administrators and the courts in establishing legislative intent.[13]

In the case of the ERA, the nature of the floor debate may be another indication of the level of external conflict and the extent to which legislators themselves had become a part of that conflict. Just as hearings provide groups with access to the media for the expansion of conflict, a fiery speech delivered during floor debate serves this same function for a legislator. Legislative participants, no less than those outside the legislature, can engage here in personal attacks upon those who disagree with them. Efforts to lower the level of conflict by placing restrictions on floor debate may be only partially successful on an issue of community conflict. Some provision for floor debate, as for hearings, may be desirable to comply with both sides' sense of "fair play" and acknowledgement of proper democratic tactics.

Texas   As befitted the routine decision which the ERA was in that state, no floor debate occurred in the Texas senate. According to the amendment's iconoclastic sponsor:

> I found out a long time ago, if you want to pass legislation then pass it. If you want to make a speech and get your name in the paper, then make a speech and have a debate.

The house engaged in only limited debate. Formal statements came from the house sponsor of the senate resolution and the original house sponsor. As the former related:

> My speech lasted about 30 seconds. I explained what Congress had done, what it was—it was an idea, a right, and a responsibility whose time had come. There were a couple of questions from the floor. Someone asked me what it was and someone asked if it would allow female-male restrooms and draft. . . . I moved off the mike [i.e., sat down] and it was a green [i.e., almost all "yes" votes on the electronic voting] board.

Considerations of time were obviously accountable in this short session, but the cursory debate was also consistent with the general absence of conflict and activity stirred on the issue within and outside the legislature.

Georgia   Floor debate on the ERA in the Georgia house in 1974 lasted part of the morning and all of the afternoon session and featured 17 speakers and numerous questions from the floor. Observers noted that it was unusual for a single piece of legislation to consume this much time in floor debate. One legislative leader, pointing to the statewide educational television network which films and replays the day's legislative debates nightly, felt the lengthiness was politically motivated:

> The television cameras were responsible for the numerous speakers on the ERA. On an issue which hits close to home, many legislators feel the need to speak to show constituents they're looking after their interests.

Proponent groups played a major role in recruiting speakers on behalf of the amendment. Legislators were seemingly reluctant to take the floor in its support. One who did speak for it explained how he came to do so:

> I spoke on the floor because I felt no one else was going to. Freshmen shouldn't get too openly involved in controversial issues and I told several supporters the previous weekend that I would not speak . . . but on the morning of the debate it looked as though it would go by default, that no one or only one or two would speak for it and this wasn't right. It would give the impression to the people of the state and country that there was little or no support for the ERA here, which is certainly not the case. And so it just sort of happened.

Amendment opponents outside the legislature reportedly played no role in recruiting floor speakers.

The speaker of the house, by not setting time limits for the debate and for individual speakers, passed up one opportunity to restrict conflict. And he may well have created an environment conducive to heightened conflict. The first speaker, the ERA sponsor, was interrupted by the sudden appearance in the house chamber of former Governor Marvin Griffin. The speaker invited the former chief executive to the stand and asked him to say a few words, which turned out to be a humorous speech against the amendment. He reported on a survey of fictitious individuals from around the state including one Willie Wireglass, who urged legislators to "consider the Constitutional Amendment carefully since women who want to join the military are free to enlist but please don't take Effie, for who in Hell will chop stovewood?" The ex-governor concluded with the maxim that "any jackass can kick the barn down but it takes a good carpenter to build one," presumably meaning that it is much easier to strike down wise legislation (as the ERA, in his opinion, would) than to write it.[14] Supporters complained afterward that it is against house rules for nonmembers to speak for or against legislation under consideration.

Although several legislative opponents confined their objections to those raised by legal scholars, many more echoed the most intemperate and irrational opponents outside the legislature. Instead of attempting to contain the controversy, several may have succeeded in expanding it even further.

One foe, a Church of God minister, said the biblical Eve was the first woman to be:

> offered power. She made a terrible mistake and caused the man to make a mistake. Many of the problems we have today have been created by the attempt of women to take power!

Another opponent, a rural legislator, shouted that the ERA "stinks of 'communism.'" He saw it as proof of communists' boast that they would take over this country without firing a shot. Then he read off a list of socialist, lesbian, and homosexual organizations which have publicly supported the ERA, an act which immediately drew the question, "If homosexuals came out for Christianity, would you say Christianity is bad?"

Comparable levity appeared again when an opponent charged the amendment would force him to hire as many women as men in his airplane business. Questions broke out on the floor about the advantages and disadvantages of that. He took his seat when one member asked him if it wouldn't "stimulate patriotism" in the Army to awaken in the morning "and find your bunkmates were somebody like Gloria Steinem and Bella Abzug."

One legislator kept assuring his neighbors, "This will legalize prostitution." Another lamented the disappearance of the suffix "man" from the English language. A third argued that with women eligible for the draft, it would be more difficult to reinstitute the draft, thereby weakening national security. Further, the ability of women soldiers to defend the country was questioned.

That such statements as the above drew ridicule from their colleagues does not imply that opponents were discredited. The fact is that the debate as a whole took place in a circus atmosphere, despite attempts by proponents to introduce a note of sobriety with reasoned presentations.[15]

Illinois   The debates on the ERA in the Illinois house have generally been held under a strictly enforced rule limiting each speaker to 10 minutes. Even so, each debate has lasted more than an hour and in 1975 it stretched to four and one-half hours. In the senate in 1972, about 2 hours were spent debating the amendment, time limitations also having been placed upon the speakers. Twenty-five senators (43 percent of the total membership) took the opportunity to speak or to explain their vote during the roll call. This indicates an extraordinary amount of interest in the ERA, even as early as May–June 1972. This amount of time, observers agreed, is typically accorded to important social issues coming before the legislature. Nor has it been necessary, as in Georgia, for interest groups to recruit floor speakers. According to one senator, "everyone wanted to speak." In the house, the sponsors have arranged the floor debate so that legislators on both sides are heard.

In the senate in 1972, those speaking in opposition during the formal debate period dealt mainly with the draft and states' rights. Only those opponents who asked for time during the roll-call to explain their votes cited constituency opinions on the traditional role of women and associated opposition arguments. It may be significant that most of the 18 senators who chose to "explain" their vote were voting in opposition. Opposition to a "women's rights" measure presumably required some explanation in Illinois.

The first house debate raised several of the more dramatic objections to the ERA: the abolition of rape and prostitution laws, unisex restrooms, sex-integrated bars, girls on football teams, and the spectre of women's liberation. Among many colorful speeches, the most infamous was that characterizing ERA's supporters outside the legislature as "bra-less, brainless broads." After a furor arose over his choice of words, the speaker claimed to have been quoted out of context. His exact words:

> We're talking about whether women want to be the same as men or women want to have equal justice. And this amendment does not say one word about justice. It says "sameness." They want women to use men's washrooms. They want women to do many of the things that for some bra-less, brainless broads that go to Washington and try to influence the Congress of the United States. . . . And these business and professional women in this state do not bake the bread. They don't do the maid work. They don't wipe the children's noses. They have nothing better to do with their time but to come and bother the legislators and the Congress of the United States with pure stupidity.

Unlike their Georgia colleagues, Illinois house members did not attempt to use God as an ally, but motherhood and the home were freely invoked by opponents during both 1972 floor debates:

> This is really an attack on the home. It's an attack on motherhood. It says that for a woman to have to be a mother and have to be a housewife is somehow degrading. I submit that problems with this society today are that the home is being attacked and assaulted and no longer wields any influence. And this is one more step, however well-intentioned the sponsors are, to attack the beauty, the sanctity, and the essentialness of having the home the center of life and society.

I suggest to you, however, that if many of our ladies had stayed in the home during the forties and didn't have to go out and work in the factories, we might not have had the violence in the 1960s that we had. And I say to you that we all love women, we want to protect them, we want them to stay like they are.

I saw in May of 1945 across the Elbe River, with my own eyes, the mixed units, male and female in the Russian Armies. . . . I personally saw an open latrine trench. I have personally seen women and men soldiers of the Russian Army squatting over those trenches. Now, visualize your daughters, your grand-daughters in that position.

Despite their leaders' attempts to restrict the conflict through rules limiting debate, Illinois legislators apparently did little more than their colleagues in Georgia to keep the conflict within bounds. In view of the fact that the conflict outside the legislature was at its lowest ebb in 1972, controversy over the ERA in Illinois was probably significantly expanded through the media attention given many of these very quotable speeches.

Proposed and Actual Policy Decisions

A common response of legislators in states where the ERA has become controversial has been to attempt to indefinitely postpone decision making. Burial or outright defeat in committee has been the most common means of doing so, but this solution has been of limited duration except in Mississippi.

Other methods have also been considered in order to avoid a decision on the amendment itself. The scheduling of a popular referendum on a proposed public policy is one such example. Even though legal precedent does not recognize state referenda as a part of the ratification process, they have been proposed in several states.

In all states where referenda have been seriously proposed, ERA proponents, fearing that distortion of the issue by the opposition could result in the amendment's defeat, have vigorously objected. Although both sides preferred to avoid the expensive statewide campaign which would be necessary, ERA opponents have tended to support these proposals. Perhaps opponents recognize that further expansion of the conflict into the community works to their advantage, given the dynamics of conflict. More likely, they are confident of victory.[16] Pressure from groups on this question, however, has probably been of less importance in persuading legislators to drop plans for referenda than the weight of legal precedent and, where a general election has been involved, legislative fears concerning running on the same ballot with such a controversial question. In the latter event, the announced positions of the legislators on the ERA would be made even more salient. A public referendum on the amendment has not been a very effective means of removing decision makers from the arena of conflict.

A related "decision not to decide" has been the submission of a state ERA to the voters.[17] Bills to place a state ERA referendum on the ballot have been introduced in several unratified states. But this alternative has been opposed by both sides even more strongly than has been a direct referendum on the federal amendment. Although a state ERA conceivably could be supported by those who base their objections to the ERA solely on the draft and states' rights issues, most opponents cannot approve any amendment which would alter protective labor legislation and domestic support laws. Proponents see few, if any, advantages to be gained. If the state ERA should fail, the federal amendment would not be ratified. If the state ERA were approved, the argument then would be that the federal amendment is not needed.[18] Again, a state ERA referendum was not viable.

A third maneuver has been the proposal of one or several pieces of legislation which would abolish specific kinds of sex discrimination. In Florida, for example, a law was passed which prohibited sex discrimination in loans and credit and guaranteed equal pay for equal work.

Whether ultimately enacted or not, these bills were meant to show the ability of legislators to respond to the needs of women without the coercion of a federal amendment. To ERA supporters, these piecemeal efforts only illustrated the need for a broad amendment redressing all forms of sex discrimination. Furthermore, it was felt that to spell out rights in a few statutory laws may imply "no rights" in areas not covered by these laws. Pro-ERA women found themselves in the strange position of working against these "women's bills" which only a year or so before would have had their full support.

Because the three approaches just discussed did not prove to be practicable, state legislatures have found another way to delay or avoid decisions on the ERA by the whole body. As in Georgia, special study committees on the ERA have been established for postponing action, at least until the following session. Group pressures can be reduced in the interim since opponents can be assured that the study committee will be a graveyard and proponents can be told that the amendment will receive the special attention that it deserves. Although the intent of the appointment of study committees or the commissioning of research on the ERA in several unratified states almost certainly was to delay or reduce the chances of future ratification, such study committees in Connecticut and Vermont may have contributed to ratification in 1973 by their favorable reports.

Texas The 1972 Texas legislature did not hesitate to act definitively and quickly on the ERA. Nor have Texas legislators, in the wake of the national controversy over the ERA, been willing to reconsider that issue. Even major lobbying efforts in 1975 and 1977 could not secure committee action on a resolution to rescind.

According to one legislator, "The attitude of most legislators was that we've got enough problems without taking this one on." Or, as one proponent outside the legislature put it:

> Politicians in this state aren't very interested in undoing things, once they're over with, and as far as this state is concerned, that issue is over with. The people voted on it and they're not interested in fooling with it.

This response to the various rescission movements in Texas at least partially explains the lack of success with which similar movements have met in other states. Decision making in the absence of conflict, as in Texas, was relatively easy. It is the rescission movement which brings conflict in its wake, and by refusing to consider resolutions to rescind in a floor vote, legislators are seeking to avoid conflict in much the same way as their colleagues in the unratified states.

Georgia   Aside from using a special study committee to delay decision making on the ERA for a year, the Georgia house did not otherwise attempt to avoid a floor vote on the amendment. Once out of committee in 1974, it was promptly brought onto the floor. On the day after its 70–104 defeat, a bill awarding women equal rights in obtaining loans and other credit was passed by the house by a vote of 168–1 in an apparent attempt to partially appease amendment supporters. In 1975, the senate also quickly defeated the ERA, 22–35. Having made these two difinitive decisions, the Georgia legislature kept the ERA in committee, 1976–78.

Illinois   Of the unratified states, the Illinois legislature has most frequently brought the ERA to the floor for a vote. (See table 5.1.) Despite the apparent willingness of Illinois legislators to make definitive decisions on the amendment, several attempts have also been made to avoid these. In 1973 a leading opponent introduced a bill providing for a referendum on the ERA on the November 1974 ballot. Because most legislators were seeking reelection then and thus were reluctant to place a controversial issue on the same ballot, the bill was tabled. In 1974, the speaker of the house introduced a resolution proposing a rules change to limit the session to fiscal bills; an ERA opponent immediately offered an amendment which would have barred *all* resolutions as well as nonfiscal bills. Failing in that, a slight effort was made among ERA opponents to prohibit reconsideration of matters discussed and defeated in past sessions. These latter two proposals were clearly designed to prevent further action on the ERA in 1974. Each, however, had a broader impact: one would have prevented the introduction of routine commemorative resolutions (e.g., honoring a person for some noteworthy accomplishment), the other would have barred lawmakers from reintroducing *all* previously defeated bills, including those sponsored as a favor to important constituents. Therefore, neither was seriously considered. A more accurate indicator of legislators' wishes to avoid definitive decision making on the ERA is the use of legislative rules in both houses to defeat the amendment.

TABLE 5.1
History of the ERA in the Illinois Legislature

Date	House Vote (N=177)		Senate Vote (N=59)	
	Yes	No	Yes	No
16 May 1972	75[1]	69		
24 May 1972			30[2]	21
15 June 1972	82[1]	76		
4 April 1973	95[3]	72		
21 May 1974			32[4]	25
18 June 1974			30[4]	24
1 May 1975	113[3]	62		
20 June 1975			28[5]	30
16 December 1976			29[5]	22
2 June 1977	101[3]	74		
7 June 1978	101[3]	64		
22 June 1978	105[3]	71		

[1] 89 votes needed for ratification.
[2] 30 votes needed for ratification.
[3] 107 votes needed for ratification (House rule).
[4] 36 votes needed for ratification (presiding officer's ruling).
[5] 36 votes needed for ratification (Senate rule).

Article XIV, Section 4 of the Illinois Constitution, adopted in 1970, requires a three-fifths majority in both houses to ratify an amendment to the state or the national constitution.[19] In 1972, however, the attorney general of Illinois issued an advisory opinion that only a simple majority was required. In 1973 the house adopted a rule requiring a three-fifths majority. Consequently, the ERA sponsors decided to try for a change of that house rule, an attempt which failed on a vote of 69 to 90, with 18 members not voting. Many legislators voted against this rules change but subsequently voted to ratify the amendment, confident that it would fail to receive a three-fifths majority. In so doing, legislators partially appeased both ERA supporters and opponents.

A similar approach to the amendment question was used by senators in 1973. More senate members had promised to support the ERA in a floor vote than were willing to vote to discharge the amendment from committee. In 1975, the same situation obtained; many senators supporting ERA voted for a rule requiring a three-fifths majority to ratify a national constitutional amendment. Although amendment supporters conceded that some legislators' votes were sincerely directed toward preserving the committee system and screening unwise amendments, other legislators, they felt, wanted to formally vote for the ERA while assuring by a second vote on procedure that their votes would not result in ratification.

FACTORS UNDERLYING THE DECISION PROCESS ON THE ERA

Behind this study is the assumption that the most telling explanations of the decision process are those based on the characteristics of interest group and community conflicts. However, the patterns of ratification in the states suggest that certain preexisting legislative cleavages (e.g., party, regional) also may have been significant determinants of nonratification. The interview data suggest additional factors, among them, sexism among male legislators and political expediency.

Party Cleavages

In Arizona, Missouri, and Illinois, Republican legislators have constituted major voting blocs against ratification. As ERA supporters in Illinois explained:

> The arguments over ERA are merely facades for a deeper enduring party division and conflict. The liberal Republicans and the independent Democrats support the ERA. The conservative Republicans oppose it. And the Daley Democrats don't give a damn, although on paper the Daley Democrats say they support it.

> The state Republican leadership for years has been ultraconservative. They fight and fear social change. The ERA has been a political issue from the day it was put on the calendar. . . . Four to six thousand bills are introduced each session and 98 percent are noncontroversial. Of those that are, a strict party line is

adopted and with ERA a strict conservative position was taken immediately. They rationalized that the Illinois Republican members of Congress didn't mean it; they mean for *us* to kill it. And that's the line they have used internally.

These partisan divisions over the ERA, however, show every evidence of masking a basic liberal-conservative split.

Personal vendettas, growing out of inter- and intraparty disputes, have also played a prominent role in the politics of the ERA in Illinois. Certain political activities of the amendment's sponsors have been linked with the defeats of 1972 through 1975. "The ERA didn't encounter difficulties; its sponsors encountered difficulties," noted one proponent group leader, who continued:

> Illinois had a bloodbath over selection of the 1972 Democratic convention delegates. . . . The key was the delegation head in selecting at-large delegates. [The Democratic House sponsor] has always been known as "independent" but in accord with the Mayor [Daley]. She's always walked that tightrope—when it's a matter of conscience, I'll do what I think is right, but why buck him on everything? She decided to buck him and voted for [Senator Adlai] Stevenson as delegation chairman and the next thing we knew, certain Daley Democratic votes, signed, sealed, and delivered, were lost. There is a direct correlation.

By 1973, Daley had reportedly forgotten this and ERA sponsors could again rely on the votes promised by his floor leader. But once more the activities of house sponsors on un-related matters contributed to defeat. Because Republicans had only a one-vote majority in the house, the Democratic leader, taking advantage of a split in Republican ranks, could have been elected speaker had he been able to get one Republican to cross over while holding all Democrats. The independent Democrats, however, chose to run their own candidate, the Democratic sponsor of the ERA. It took eight ballots before a Republican was finally elected, and on some ballots the Democratic sponsor received votes from Republicans strongly committed to the advancement of women in politics. The speaker was felt to have remembered this when he ruled that a three-fifths majority was required for ratification.

In 1975 there was considerable speculation that Mayor Daley was obstructing a vote on the ERA in the senate (after house ratification) until the house passed his congressional reapportionment plan. Furthermore, the senate sponsor and the mayor's son, Senator Richard Daley, were engaged in a political power struggle.

Although these particular partisan disputes were no doubt factors in the defeat of the ERA in Illinois, it is likely that had the amendment not been the subject of statewide controversy, its sponsors would have been punished in some other way.

Regionalism

The resistance of the southern states[20] can, in large measure, be explained in terms of the ideological distinctiveness of that region. According to this view, the romantic southern ideal that men are meant to wield power and women are to be protected and idolized has assured a cool reception for the amendment in the South. It is further argued that girls in the South are more rigidly socialized into the traditional female role and, when married, show an unusually strong sense of duty to family coupled with a deep religious sentiment.[21] However, this more traditional view of the role of women in society is only one manifestation of a generally conservative approach to social change.

Legislative Attitudes toward the Role of Women

Not only were societal views on the role of women linked with decisions on the ERA, but the individual attitudes of legislators on that topic were also frequently cited by legislators and group leaders in their attempts to explain these decisions. In Texas, the personal attitudes of the legislator—the ways in which he viewed women—were considered more important than his basic political orientation. "There are about ten mossbacks who will oppose any female rights bill," confided one legislator. Another said, "There are still X number of men who think 'home, cooking' is where a woman is supposed to be."

In Georgia, several legislators, including some opponents, felt the primary reason for ERA legislative opposition was the fact that legislators did not want to remove women from the prestigious position ("the pedestal") they now hold. A proponent leader was more blunt; she blamed rural legislators who want to keep their women barefoot and pregnant. The wives of male legislators also influenced their husbands on this issue. One legislator noted that many colleagues had confessed to him that they were under instructions from their wives to oppose the ERA.[22] Another Georgia proponent commented:

> They [the legislators] are afraid of what ERA may lead to, coupled with a basic fear of women. They *want* to believe that women are different by nature. They don't want to think of women as legal people. . . . There's a lot of very insecure men around.

Illinois supporters were even more outspoken concerning male prejudice. A woman identified as a leading organizer for the ERA exclaimed:

> What can we do against such male chauvinists? The men are so afraid we may get some of their power away from them, that society will be changed overnight.[23]

This analysis was echoed by others, who felt that some male legislators' view of the proper role of women in society was the basic problem, compounded by their own insecurity and that of their wives. One legislator suggested that:

> We're still afraid of what we don't know but basically it has to do with the feelings of the role of the female in society. The men who are opposed are insecure and threatened. . . . The men in the legislature who are the strongest opponents are the Don Juan types who need a lot of scalps on their belts, who are basically very insecure in their relationships with women.

This shifting of responsibility for the defeat of the ERA in Georgia and Illinois from relatively impersonal legal issues surrounding the ERA to very personal characteristics of the legislators themselves may be attributed simply to the normal dynamics of a community conflict. Certainly the proponents' explanation of legislative reponses to the ERA contains elements of personal slander and direct hostility often observed by those studying such conflicts. But the possibility that the ERA, as a woman's issue, *has* brought the personal attitudes of male legislators into the decision process cannot be dismissed either. Male chauvinism may well have combined with a generally conservative approach to issues of public policy to prevent ratification.

The ERA as an Ideological Conflict

Certainly, participants in the ERA controversy in Illinois and Georgia did not dismiss the importance of the disagreement between liberals and conservatives in the legislature over the amendment. All agreed that the most effective supporting arguments were the basic justice of granting legal equality to American women and the moral obligation of representatives to protect *all* people, arguments of particular appeal to those of liberal dispositions. Those on both sides conceded that many legislative supporters were motivated by a deep philosophical belief in the "rightness" of the ERA.

The issues on which members of the legislature based their opposition were much the same in Georgia and Illinois, with only a difference in emphasis. In Georgia, the issue of states' rights was linked with hostility toward the Supreme Court and fear of the Court's interpretation of the amendment. As one supporter noted, "Who could have predicted in 1954 that the Brown decision would lead to massive busing in 1974?" Participants in Illinois denied there was any real antagonism toward the Supreme Court behind ERA opposition. Rather, states' rights advocates there argued that the Fourteenth Amendment was adequate to protect women under the Constitution. The ERA, they felt, would merely remove the power of state legislatures "to legislate on men and women and transfer this to the courts, the least responsible branch of government."

The issue of the draft and, by extension, national security, was also of concern to many legislators in both states. Georgia supporters felt that the draft was the strongest opposition issue and that the allegation that women would not be capable of protecting the country was the most damaging argument heard during the floor debate. The draft was the most commonly mentioned objection to the ERA in Illinois as well. A leading legislative opponent confessed that he had switched to the opposition only after he came to realize that the "ERA would lead to a radical restructuring of our views toward women in the military."

The question of altered conditions of military service for women under the ERA is one which has given proponents the most difficulty. Aside from the issue of women in combat, expanded opportunities for women in the military has inspired questions regarding finances (e.g., the cost of altering ships and barracks to provide privacy), national security (i.e., the inability of women to defend the country), and the future of the draft and volunteer army (i.e., the unwillingness of women to bear arms). All these issues are of deep concern to political conservatives.

Political liberals have more readily agreed that "with equal rights goes equal responsibility," an argument applying not only to military service for women but also to domestic support and conditions of employment outside the home. But advocacy of the special treatment of women, in law, if not in fact, in these three areas is deeply entrenched in many sectors of society and is reflected in the votes of many legislators.

There also appeared to be a strong undercurrent of conservative resistance to social change in general. This was evident in the response of an Illinois legislator who objected to the expense of revising laws to bring them into compliance with the amendment. Another compared the opponents' homemade apple pies to "our laws that have taken years to build."[24]

The ERA, as a broad policy of general and enduring social import, is the kind of issue which can easily be converted into a full-scale conflict. When it was before Congress, the amendment was viewed as a legal issue and was discussed in abstract and technical terms by supporters and opponents. Once the ratification process began, the ERA was redefined into much broader terms by opponents in order to actively involve many subgroups of the population in the conflict. The debate became more concrete, graphic, and nontechnical, and expanded to include issues unrelated (or just barely related) to the ERA. At its height, the ERA conflict has been fueled by differences in attitudes among individuals (both in the public at large and the state legislatures) concerning government, society, and social change.

The Dynamics of Conflict

Although the ERA was tailor-made for a controversy fought along liberal-conservative lines, the dynamics of conflict itself, once set into motion, guaranteed that it be ratified only with difficulty, if at all. As is true in most community conflicts, the opposition to the ERA, once mobilized, sustained much of its initial effectiveness.

There is no clear pattern for all unratified and late-ratifying states concerning changes in the level of conflict from one year to the next. In some states where little interest was shown in the ERA within or outside the legislature in 1973, conflict dramatically increased in the 1974 session. In other states where the conflict was intense in 1973, debate was restrained in 1974. On the whole, proponents there claimed to have picked up support in the legislature in 1974 as the level of opposition activity declined, the debating died down, and the emotional arguments against the ERA were effectively countered. Even so, there was sufficient opposition in the legislature in 1974 to block ratification in all but three of the (then) twenty unratified states.

Texas   As one Texas journalist has observed, "When the Equal Rights Amendment to the U.S. Constitution was passed by Texas . . . it raised about as much interest as a sewer bond referendum."[25] Although the state ELRA had for many years been highly controversial within the legislature, it was approved in April 1971. The federal amendment, coming in its wake, passed without any conflict at all. As one legislator recalled:

> ERA ratification in Texas was very low-key. There just wasn't much involved in it. It wasn't emotional; it was not highly contested.

Georgia   Legislators agreed the amendment was one of the most controversial issues the Georgia legislature had faced in recent sessions. Furthermore, the debating had become irrational. As one legislator put it:

> The ERA became so filled with emotion in Georgia that common sense didn't prevail. I heard a lot of legislators say, "Just don't confuse me with any facts."

In retrospect, supporters outside the legislature expressed different opinions about the consequences of the conflict for ratification in Georgia. Some (a small majority) thought the ERA would have been ratified in 1972 had the legislature been in session, an opinion echoed by one opponent as well. Others, noting that Georgia did not ratify the Nineteenth Amendment until 1970 ("That indicates where they stand about women."), discounted ERA's chances in 1972. They were in agreement, however, that the dramatic appearance of the opposition in January 1973, sounded the death knell for ratification that year.

With the exception of one legislator who saw no difference in the aggregate support for the ERA in the house, 1973–74 (only a few individual changes of opinion in both directions), legislators and group leaders on both sides of the issue concurred that the ERA picked up support in the 1974 session after the initial impact of the opposition campaign in 1973. The most frequently mentioned figure was 20 votes. More legislators were also willing to publicly support the amendment during the 1974 session. The sudden appearance of the opponents in 1973 had not only caused many legislators to switch from support to opposition, but had also neutralized several supporters. Following the national pattern, the Georgia legislature and ERA's supporters outside the legislature were somewhat better able to deal with the controversy in 1974.

Illinois Although one Illinois legislator felt the ERA was surpassed by gun control as an issue involving passion and stimulating mail, most of his colleagues agreed that the amendment has been a very emotional issue. According to its sponsor:

> There's never been any issue which generated even one-tenth of the reaction, whether enthusiasm or hostility. This is true of constituents all over the state. I previously had worked on environmental issues, health, education, rights of children, good government. I never had worked on anything which generated such crackling hostility among my fellow legislators.

As in Georgia, the initial appearance of opposition to the amendment had a profound effect on legislative support for the ERA in the Illinois house of representatives. As a sponsor recalls:

> We had 95 cosponsors for the ERA in 1972. We went around and collected signatures. It was an equal rights amendment and they saw the leaders were behind it and they all said, "Fine." But when time came for the vote, even the cosponsors didn't vote for it because in the interim they'd had a chance to have a reaction set in and they heard from the opposition. . . . It's difficult to judge whether this was the opposition mobilizing or a gut reaction on the part of men had had a chance to set in, which was then fed by the opposition women.[26]

If the raw vote totals are used as criterion, then support for the ERA, 1972–78, has been constant in the senate and has increased dramatically in the house. Many activists, including several opponents, feel these roll-call votes *are* accurate indicators of existing support. Several credit this to the work of supporters outside the legislature.

One legislator, however, denied that the votes were indicative of growing strength. He felt instead that they were a function of the three-fifths rule, which allowed some legislators to vote for it, knowing that support would fall below that required for ratification. Some participants denied that any real change in legislative support for the ERA had occurred over time; with the exception of a few conversions here and there, most legislators had not changed their positions. Others, particularly legislators, felt the ERA had actually lost support. The repeated failures to ratify had created their own momentum. Legislators were beginning to say that if the ERA failed again, they would not support it the next time it was brought up. And in fact this observation has been corroborated in the voting since June 1975.

The dynamics of conflict over the ERA appear to form a pattern. Opponents have been most effective in preventing ratification at the outset of their campaign. They have been able to create a reasonable doubt in the minds of some legislators; preexisting favorable opinions on the ERA have been reversed. After the initial impact of the opposition has been felt, supporters have been able to at least partially recoup their losses in the legislature by vigorous lobbying and rational explanation. If the issue is considered in several sessions, however, the advantage may again shift to the opposition, as legislators grow impatient to deal with new issues.

Political Expediency

The interest group conflict model, however, suggests that a long period of debate over an issue does not necessarily favor opponents. With conflict, the decision process is slowed to allow legislators to weigh the relative strengths of opposing groups. The politically stronger group, whether supporters or opponents of the issue, is most effective in influencing decision makers.

As has been noted, political expediency was believed to be a factor in the decisions of some legislators to support the amendment. Future electoral success was linked with support of the ERA by at least some legislators. The three-fifths rule allowed certain Illinois legislators, personally opposed to the ERA, to go on record in its support. In Georgia, where genuine legislative support for the amendment was lower than in Illinois, it was widely noted that when the house voted on the ERA in 1974, relatively few "green" (yes) lights initially appeared on the voting board. Quickly, before the voting apparatus was locked, several legislators switched their votes to support the amendment on the official count. Georgia supporters admitted that, had the vote been closer initially, many of these changes would not have occurred. As one legislator explained:

> When the issue is hot, the winners look at the total and walk away happy. The losers look at the individual votes and get bitter.

The important point here is that rarely was it asserted that legislative *opposition* to the amendment, as contrasted with support, was a matter of political expediency. This suggests that were the interest group model of conflict a perfect predictor of legislative responses of the ERA, ratification would have been achieved in both states. Supporters were perceived as more politically influencial and important than opponents.

In Texas, in the absence of organized opposistion, it was assumed that the ERA was wanted by *all* women and that legislators could deny these demands only at their own peril.

The timing of the ratification was considered important, coming as it did shortly before the 1972 party primaries. Remarked a supporter:

> I think if the legislature had had time to think about it, they wouldn't have done it so fast. But this was an election spring for them; they were all going back to run in the 1972 Democratic or Republican primary.

One legislator, an opponent, confirmed that many legislators were not inherently in favor of the amendment but that it became an election issue. Two legislators also observed that the state ELRA had long been used by some legislators to organize women behind them. In private, they laughed about the state amendment, mocking its female supporters.

Summary and Conclusions

Legislative responses to the ERA can be divided into two categories: those decisions made in the absence of conflict and those made amidst conflict after the appearance of organized opposition to the amendment. In the case of the former, ratification was often handled like a routine decision. Several steps in the legislative process were omitted as rules were suspended, committees were by-passed, and hearings were not scheduled. Nor were legislators interested in holding extensive floor debates before ratifying. After the opposition to the amendment was mobilized, however, the legislative histories of the ERA reveal a succession of maneuvers to protract the convoluted process of legislating as long as possible. Legislative efforts to restrict the conflict, if attempted at all, were only partially successful.

Many decision makers were neutralized by the development of conflict, which sometimes meant that the most influential legislators were unwilling to sponsor the ERA. Some legislators became opponents of the amendment and active participants in the conflict on account of doubts concerning the amendment planted by the opposition movement.

Decision makers also at times attempted to avoid decision making. In this, however, they were thwarted by the peculiar conditions surrounding the ratification of any constitutional amendment and the ERA in particular. A public referendum on the latter was not viable for both legal and political reasons. Nor were the alternative approaches for providing legal equality for women—statutory revision and a state ERA—acceptable to groups outside the legislature. Both also required a legislative commitment to eliminate sex discrimination that may have been lacking.

Use of the committee system to avoid decision making only slowed the decision process in most unratified or late-ratifying states. Eventually, the ERA reached the floor. In only three states was the ERA initially kept in committee for more than one year; only in Mississippi has the ERA continued to remain in committee since 1972. As a rule, pressure on committee members from proponent groups to release the amendment was too intense for committees to continue to willingly shield their colleagues from the conflict.

The presence of conflict introduces a bias against the adoption of any new policy, and although the lines of legislative division over the ERA coincided with previously existing cleavages—interparty, intraparty, ideological—it was the statewide conflict which caused these cleavages to be salient here.

Before conflict arose, interest group pressures were (or were perceived to be) exerted only in support of the amendment. In accordance with these pressures, ratification quickly followed. The initial appearance of the opposition had a negative effect upon the likelihood of ERA ratification. And even though legislative support for it, as shown by roll-call votes, has since increased, opponents have maintained much of their effectiveness in preventing further ratifications. Those studying other community conflicts have noted that initial decisions on controversial issues are rarely reversed; this seems to be only partially applicable to the history of the ERA in the states. Several states have ratified the ERA after initial rejection. One force working against repeated failures to ratify is the general agreement that political expediency requires legislative support for the ERA.

The decision process on the ERA in Texas illustrates the importance of political expediency in the absence of conflict.

The legislature there expedited consideration of the amendment with the support of legislative leaders and influential sponsors. The amendment was ratified by large majorities in both houses.

The Georgia legislature seemingly was more deeply affected by the conflict over the ERA than was the Illinois legislature. Key persons and groups—legislative leaders, the sponsor and potential sponsors, legislative supporters, the committee considering the amendment itself— were neutralized. Hearings and floor debate were both lengthy and highly emotional. With the rejection of the amendment in both houses, 1974–75, no further action has been taken on it.

Illinois legislators were more successful in managing conflict through the use of procedural rules regulating debate and hearings. Committees were by-passed in order to bring the ERA to the floor for a vote. Floor debate after 1972 avoided the most emotion-laden and peripheral issues. Even so, the Illinois legislature, too, was deeply affected by the conflict. This was evident in the problems of sponsorship, the split among the legislative leadership, obstructionist committees, and the number of participants in the floor debates. The legislature also was able to prevent ratification through rules changes requiring a three-fifths majority.

Georgia, in rejecting the ERA, conformed to a southern regional pattern of policy making on this issue. In Illinois, where a strongly competitive political party system exists, interparty and intraparty disputes had a notable impact on ERA ratification. The basic reason for nonratification in both states, however, is that the statewide conflict over the ERA caused many legislators to look beyond the narrow legal merits of the amendment and instead to base their votes on personal attitudes on government, society, social change, and the proper role of women.

NOTES

1. Twenty-two of the 32 state legislatures meeting in 1972 after March 22 ratified. Of the 10 unratified states, 3 took no action; in 2 the ERA was ratified in the lower house, with the senate failing to act; in 3 more, the upper house ratified and the lower house rejected the amendment; in 2 states the lower house rejected the amendment,

with the senate failing to act. Thus in only 5 states was the ERA actually defeated in a floor vote.

2. Jeane J. Kirkpatrick, *Political Woman* (New York: Basic, 1974), p. 124.

3. His opposition to the state ELRA revolved around preservation of state community property laws. As he interpreted the ERA, these laws would remain intact because "it's a federal amendment." In the light of this misconception, the opponents of the ERA may be correct in some individual cases when they assert that "legislators didn't know what they were voting on" in 1972.

4. Sponsorship in the senate also proved to be a problem in 1975. Lt. Gov. Zell Miller was attempting to form a broad-based coalition to sponsor the amendment when the controversial black civil rights activist Julian Bond, among others, independently introduced a resolution to ratify. It was generally felt that Bond's sponsorship reduced support for the ERA.

5. Under the rules of the Texas legislature, the presiding officer can refer a bill or resolution to any committee.

6. The loose coalition of groups working for the ERA in Georgia agreed that even defeat in the full house was preferable to death in committee. However, one member, the representative of two large women's groups, acting alone, wrote a letter requesting that the ERA be kept in committee to build additional support for it in the interim. This was done, and the letter was presented by the sponsor as representing all proponents' wishes.

7. The Senate Judiciary Committee has been less reluctant to engage in decision making. In 1975, the resolution was approved and sent to the floor. In 1977, it was kept in subcommittee but was promptly brought up and defeated the following year.

8. Gilbert Y. Steiner and Samuel K. Gove, *Legislative Politics in Illinois* (Urbana: University of Illinois Press, 1960), pp. 61–62.

9. David Kenney, *Basic Illinois Government: A Systematic Explanation* (Carbondale: Southern Illinois University Press, 1970), p. 154.

10. David B. Truman, *The Governmental Process* (New York: Knopf, 1951), p. 372.

11. Jo Freeman, *The Politics of Women's Liberation* (New York: Longman, 1975), p. 224.

12. Subsequently, senate hearings were held in 1975 (two days) and 1977 (two hours). Both sets of hearings were well attended and very heated.

13. Charles L. Clapp, *The Congressman: His Work as He Sees It* (Garden City, N.Y.: Doubleday, 1963), pp. 140–41; Donald R. Matthews, *U.S. Senators and Their World* (New York: Vintage, 1960), pp. 247–49.

14. This scene is reminiscent of the episode in the Tennessee house on the opening day of the 1974 session during which the ERA was rescinded. Legislators were treated to a 10-minute skit when the speaker suspended the rules. Based roughly on the legend of Rip Van Winkle, the skit featured a post-ERA society where women were drafted for front-line duty, paid alimony, did manual labor, and played profes-

sional football. The skit ended with men and women going away hand-in-hand to the restroom.

15. Newspaper accounts indicate that the debate in the senate in 1975 was more subdued. The issue of states' rights seemed to be of primary concern to senate opponents.

16. If state referenda on a state ERA provide a reliable index, opponents are not necessarily so advantaged. In only 4 states—Wisconsin (1973), New York (1975), New Jersey (1975), and Florida (1978)—has a state ERA been defeated at the polls. In 12 other states since 1970, voters have approved a state ERA or a constitution containing such a provision. Most recently, in November 1974, voters in Connecticut and New Hampshire added ERA's to their constitutions, as did Massachusetts in 1976.

17. Ironically, several ratifying states have since added, or have attempted to add, an ERA to their own state constitutions, having recognized an immediate need for such.

18. There are three unratified states—Illinois, Virginia, and Utah—which already had equal rights provisions in their constitutions before the submission of the federal ERA.

19. In 1975 a federal appeals court held that this requirement is not binding and that each house can make its own rules regarding the adoption of constitutional amendments.

20. Included here are also states with cultural ties to the South, such as Missouri and Oklahoma.

21. Roy Reed, "In the South, Road to Equal Rights Is Rocky and Full of Detours," New York Times, 20 March 1975, p. 51.

22. Former Congresswoman and ERA sponsor Martha Griffiths has noted that most legislators are relatively affluent married men with wives who do not work. This results in a legislative bias, since the perspective of single people and working couples is omitted. New Orleans Times-Picayune, 19 January 1975.

23. Chicago Tribune, 12 June 1974.

24. One measure of conservatism used in survey research is agreement with the statement, "If something grows up over a long time, there will always be much wisdom in it."

25. "The Ladies Mobilize," The Texas Observer 16 (November 1974): 1–5.

26. This explanation is somewhat at odds with that pertaining to the 1972 Democratic party dispute, discussed on pp. 167–68.

Epilogue

This study is, unfortunately, similar to a mystery novel with the concluding chapter missing, because, as of this writing, time still remains for the amendment to be ratified. The conflict could be ultimately resolved in several ways. Three more states could ratify the amendment before March 22, 1979.[1] It is also possible that with the successful campaign to extend the deadline for ratification, the conflict will continue beyond 1979.[2] Or perhaps the ERA will go the way of the Child Labor Amendment,[3] which was never ratified by the requisite number of states, but whose basic principle was instead adopted into national and state law. Instead of a conclusion, then, there is only an epilogue providing a few further comments.

Certainly the eventual resolution of the ERA conflict involves high stakes for both sides. The amendment's success or failure has been pictured as a litmus test of the new feminist movement. The defeat of state ERA referenda in New York and New Jersey in November 1975 brought on a rash of stories questioning, "Does the Women's Movement Still Have Clout?" Some feel that the ERA must be ratified or women may again be deemed "of aesthetic appeal rather than political import."[4]

In an effort to achieve ratification before March 22, 1979, and also to demonstrate political clout, the National Organization for Women in 1977 called for an economic boycott of unratified states. By August 1978, 202 organizations had voted to hold their conventions only in states that had ratified. It has been estimated that in excess of $100 million in convention business over the next several years has been transferred from cities such as Chicago, Kansas City, Las Vegas, Miami, Atlanta, and New Orleans.[5]

The ERA has also been an important issue for recruiting new members into the contending groups, much as was the issue of women's suffrage during the period 1890–1920. The publicity accorded the present pro-ERA women's groups during this conflict attracted many women to all supporting groups, but particularly to the new feminist organizations. Each failure of a legislature to ratify the amendment reportedly brought in its wake many new proponent group members enraged at such dereliction. The rapid growth of the National Organization for Women, for example, has caused concern among some NOW leaders that the women's movement could rapidly decline following ERA ratification, much as the suffrage movement was unable to channel its membership into new activities after 1920.

Groups opposed to the ERA also share the concern with demonstrating political clout and attracting (and holding) new members. Pointing to the entry of the John Birch Society into active opposition to the amendment, an official of the Anti-Defamation League noted:

> There is no doubt that the John Birch Society only latched onto ERA when they sensed an issue they could exploit. The Society is always looking for an issue of this kind that has popular appeal and can bring them into contact with segments of opinion in the mainstream.[6]

It is felt that many amendment opponents have been interested in organizing women for participation in political conflicts in addition to that over ERA. With the appearance of the so-called New Right in the mid-1970s, this interpretation of the opposition's underlying motivations assumes greater credence. The ERA has emerged as one of the key issues uniting this new conservative political movement.[7]

Given the importance attached to the matter by both sides, the conflict over the ERA represents a fascinating clash of two important and powerful social movements. And the history of ERA ratification in the states indicates that both models of political conflict used in this study are quite accurately descriptive of certain aspects of the struggle. Before opposition to the ERA arose, legislators and proponent groups acted solely according to the interest group model of conflict, and the amendment was ratified with high legislative consensus. Since then, ratification has involved community, rather than strictly intergroup, conflict in almost all late-ratifying and unratified states. Deviations from the community conflict model in these states can be traced to three sources: level of government, type of group participant, and type of issue.

Level of Government   When the site of conflict is an entire state rather than a single city, the personal characteristics associated with participants in such a conflict change. Even though the opposition was less emotionally restrained than proponents in the arguments it used, the anti-ERA leaders were of a higher social status and had greater political experience than the community conflict model would suggest. These greater skills were needed to organize and coordinate a statewide movement. Yet, because of the anonymity afforded by strategy emphasizing mail and literature distribution, leaders did not risk greatly their standing in the community. Thus, their relatively high social status did not, in this case, constrain opposition leaders.

The heavy reliance by both sides on traditional interest group tactics as well can be attributed to the level of government involved. There is a set of generally recognized procedures for influencing state legislators. More important, several of the members of established groups, active on both sides, were already familiar with these methods from their participation in earlier lobbying campaigns.

Type of Group Participant   The type of group involved also contributes to an admixture of characteristics of interest group and community conflicts. Many of the groups backing the ERA had long-standing commitments to the amendment, which were reinforced by a high degree of internal consensus. Established groups are neutralized by conflicts only when internal disunity over the issue threatens group survival. This condition did *not* obtain in the case of the ERA. And as established groups, many of them long active in legislative lobbying, they clung to most of the conventional lobbying methods. Yet, as women's groups, they lacked many of the advantages of other interest groups: partisan alignments, committee linkages, experience with intergroup coalitions.

As women's groups, seeking to speak for over 50 percent of the population, both sides predictably had greater difficulties in establishing their legitimacy than did groups claiming to represent a narrow constituency. The opposition had some success in portraying ERA proponents as an unrepresentative elite. Those testifying against the amendment often noted they were members of groups formally or actively in support of the ERA. The grass-roots membership, they charged, was never polled concerning the official endorsement. With even greater effect, opponents were able to distort the broad base of support for the ERA. In the minds of a sizable segment of the general public and many legislators, the ERA became associated exclusively with NOW and "the radical feminists." The broad pro-ERA coalition thus was transformed into an elitist minority fringe indifferent to homemakers and low-salaried women workers and who would force all women out of the home and into jobs.

In comparison with supporters, opposition forces were not handicapped by the image they projected. Many anti-ERA leaders had been active in politics before the ERA conflict arose. They were often well-educated, middle to upper middle-class, articulate spokespersons for their politically conservative viewpoints. As such, state legislators could not easily disregard them. Nor were the media willing to stifle even the least decorous element of the opposition by denying them access to a public forum. It is also clear that many proponents, just as were the opponents, were not always constrained by the conventional political rules of the game. For example, the National Organization for Women, formed during a period of confrontation tactics, resorted to these methods when the ERA met with opposition in the states.

Type of Issue   The explanatory power of the existing community conflict model was also altered by the type of policy the ERA represents. As a constitutional amendment, it was nonamendable, thus presenting both sides with an "all or nothing" situation. As a constitutional amendment, it was also couched in sufficiently broad language to be subject to varying interpretations and to be easily distorted. Further, the subject of equal legal rights for women raised questions touching upon certain very basic social values.

All the above characteristics encouraged community conflict. However, because a constitutional amendment was involved, legislators had fewer options in avoiding or postponing decision making. A nondecision was impossible; there was no way a proposed amendment to the U.S. Constitution could be kept off the legislative agenda indefinitely. Nor were "decisions not to decide" easy here. Robbed of the device of the popular referendum, legislators themselves eventually had to make a definitive decision. Since the ERA was considered by every state at about the same time, the actions of one state could readily affect those of another. This interactive effect no doubt worked to the disadvantage of proponents after 1973. However, the peculiar dynamics of the constitutional amendment ratification process may have slowed the development of an effective opposition in 1972. States, in particular the smaller states, are ordinarily eager to be included among the early ratifiers of a new amendment. Thus, the bandwagon effect initially worked to the advantage of ERA ratification.

Despite idiosyncratic lapses in explaining the course of ERA ratification, the community conflict model accurately described many aspects of the ERA controversy. The conflict was intially introduced into the states by a national opposition force. Ad hoc groups, usually opposed to the amendment, were formed to contest the issue. The local media played a role in publicizing the conflict and in legitimizing the opposition. Local and state elites, though only rarely neutralized by the dispute, may have hurt the ERA by their failure to actively support it.

The original disputed points pertaining to the amendment underwent a great transformation as members of the general public were drawn into the conflict. Those actively backing the ERA were disadvantaged in that those in the general public who initially favored the ERA were not always deeply committed. Women often felt that their life patterns were set unalterably and that the ERA would not be of much personal value. Potential benefits also seemed small in comparison with the possible upheavals envisioned by opponents. Not being deeply committed to the ERA, these persons could change their opinion without violating their need for internal consistency.

Opponents made it quite easy to reverse a once favorable opinion on the ERA by representing the amendment in symbols posing a threat to traditional beliefs and values. Different persons and groups worried about different parts of the ERA's projected consequences, shaping a formidable negative coalition.

Backers found it hard to convince people of the merits of a proposal as complex as the ERA. Instead of stressing the concrete benefits to be gained with ratification, supporters often displayed the amendment as a moral imperative. Nor was it easy to spell out the possible eventualities of the ERA since as a constitutional amendment it is meant to establish a broad principle offering guidance to legislators and the courts.

Constitutional scholars, ostensibly the "experts" on the ERA's impact, were unable to lend rationality to the debate. Knowledgeable lawyers often declined to discuss the subject in a public forum for fear their words later would be twisted, as were the law review articles by Paul Freund and Thomas Emerson et al.[8] For example, a group of University of Chicago law professors, including the noted constitutional scholar Phillip Kurland, were known to be in opposition to the amendment. Yet all refused to appear on local television. As Gresham's Law of Conflict correctly states, the harmful and dangerous elements drive out those who would keep the conflict within bounds. Because those with genuine expertise often refused to participate in the debate, each side portrayed its own spokespersons as "experts," and this definition was, in general, not challenged in the larger community.

In short, amendment proponents won when they faced no opposition. Opponents, usually but not always, won simply by getting their message through to legislators and to the general public. The relationship here between group activities and governmental decision making on an issue of state-wide conflict suggests several general patterns of political behavior:

1. In the wake of conflict, highly committed and consensual groups will not be neutralized. However, organizations for whom the issue is not central to group purposes (e.g., in the case of the ERA, labor unions) will not be actively involved in the dispute. Formal, but not active, commitments will be a common response of state and local leaders as well.

2. The leadership of both parties in a conflict is drawn from a common pool of politically experienced, relatively high-status members of established groups. Only if politically effective interest groups are not available to contest the issue will ad hoc organizations be formed.

3. At the height of a public conflict, decision makers respond primarily to the conflict itself and are unable to differentiate between the tactics, political strengths, and principal arguments of both sides. As a result, neither side may be perceived as legitimate.

4. In the presence of conflict, decision makers seek to avoid definitive actions on the issue. Some become neutralized by the conflict; others switch sides to become active opponents of the proposed issue.

5. With conflict, preexisting cleavages in the decision-making body—partisan, intraparty, ideological—become germane. In the absence of conflict, such divisions have little or no bearing in decision making on the issue.

6. However, in those states where one party to a conflict has considerably greater political strength and is perceived by decision makers as capable of removing officials through the election process, decision makers may ignore preexisting cleavages to support that group's position.

In retrospect, the possibility presents itself that the ERA was introduced prematurely into the states. It may be yet another example of "future shock," wherein the individual feels overwhelmed by modern society. As the theme from the popular television show, "All in the Family" notes, "You knew what you were then; girls were girls and men were men." The individual feels that self-determination has been lost, that changes which he/she does not understand are being imposed by remote institutions over whom he/she has no control. For such people, rejection of the ERA may have represented an opportunity to symbolically say "no" to all such disruptions.

Although the Equal Rights Amendment was by no means a new issue in 1972—it had been before Congress since 1923—public knowledge about it was minimal. The new feminist movement had only begun to gain public awareness and acceptance; note the increased support within the general public for efforts to strengthen or change women's status in society, 1970–74 (see table 2.6). Had proponents waited only until 1974 to push for congressional passage, it is possible that ratification would have been treated as routine and quietly adopted nationwide. At the very least, much of the uncertainty concerning the amendment's consequences for existing laws might have been removed. It was hoped that the release in 1976 of reports from governors' offices on the impact of the state ERA's then in force would serve this purpose. These shed a positive light on the federal ERA by challenging opposition charges that the ERA is unnecessary, costly, and detrimental. However, by 1976, the ERA had already come to be characterized as controversial, members of the general public had joined in the conflict, decision makers had become wary, and a pattern of legislative defeats had been established.

NOTES

1. Should the courts choose to rule on this question and uphold the rescission resolutions which have been passed, or should Congress break with precedent to recognize these resolutions as valid, ratification by more than three states would be needed.
2. On October 20, 1977, Rep. Elizabeth Holtzman (D.-N.Y.) introduced a resolution which would have extended the deadline for ratification from March 22, 1979, to March 22, 1986. Citing two Court decisions—*Dillon* v. *Gloss* 256 U.S. 994 (1921) and *Coleman* v. *Miller* 307 U.S. 433 (1939)—and Article I, Section 8 of the U.S. Constitution (the "necessary and proper" clause), the Justice Department advised Congress that it has the power to extend the deadline by a simple majority vote. On August 15, 1978, the House of Representatives approved, by a vote of 233–189, a 39-month extension (to June 30, 1982). On October 6, the Senate concurred, 60–36.
3. The so-called Child Labor Amendment was proposed to the states by the Congress in June 1924. No specific time limitation was established for its ratification, so theoretically it still could be ratified. However,

between 1924 and 1936 the amendment was rejected by the legislatures of 26 states and ratified in only 5.

4. Graham Wootten, *Interest-Groups* (Englewood Cliffs, N.J.: Prentice-Hall, 1970), p. 42.
5. *National NOW Times* (11 March 1978): 1.
6. Quoted in Lisa Cronin Wohl, "White Gloves and Combat Boots: The Fight for ERA," *Civil Liberties Review* 1 (Fall 1974): 79.
7. Others are opposition to abortion, affirmative action, sex education, gay rights, busing, gun control, the Panama Canal Treaties, national health insurance, unionization of the military, and the Strategic Arms Limitations Talks (SALT).
8. Paul Freund, "The Equal Rights Amendment Is Not the Way," *Harvard Civil Rights–Civil Liberties Law Review* 6 (March 1971): 234–42; Thomas I. Emerson et al., "The Equal Rights Amendment: A Constitutional Basis for Equal Rights for Women," *Yale Law Journal* 80 (April 1971): 871–985.

Appendix A

Home State, Sex, and Role of Study Participants

Role	Texas	Georgia	Illinois
Legislator			
Male			
Proponent	4	4	1
Opponent	4	2	4
Female			
Proponent	1	2	3
Opponent	0	0	1
Group leader			
Male			
Proponent	3	0	2
Opponent	1	3	0
Female			
Proponent	7	10	10
Opponent	1	4	8
Other Influentials			
Male			
Proponent	0	1	0
Opponent	0	0	0
Female			
Proponent	1	1	0*
Opponent	0	0	0
TOTAL (N = 78)	22	27	29

*The chairperson of the Illinois Commission on the Status of Women in 1974 was also a legislator.

Appendix B

Interview Guide for Group Leaders and Other Activists in Equal Rights Amendment Ratification

Coalitions and Activities

1. How did you get involved in ERA ratification? (Establish whether this was through a group membership and the date of initial involvement.)

2. Are you or your group associated with one of the coalitions working for (against) ratification? (If so, establish the date of formation and who individually or as a group took the initiative.)

3. Which groups or individuals belong to the coalition? (Also determine if any groups or individuals were deliberately excluded or if some were particularly recruited, such as Catholics, labor, fundamentalists, housewives, men, farm groups, blacks, or low-income groups.)

4. How does the coalition operate? That is, what kind of formal organization exists for working for (against) ratification? (Establish the contribution members make in terms of grass-roots support, money, labor, and professional lobbyists; help received from national headquarters and the ERA Ratification Council; formal task forces and communication networks established.)

5. Have you ever worked for or against the passage of a bill in the state legislature before? (Establish the level of political activism of the respondent in the past as well as that of his/her co-workers. Establish if those most active here on the ERA are group leaders with formal positions, rank-and-file members who are especially interested in the ERA and perhaps came into the group because of it,

or are without a group affiliation. Probe for the educational and occupational status of those on this side of the ERA dispute.)

6. In general, is there any disagreement on tactics which has to be worked out? (Determine if new feminist groups and traditional groups are split on tactics.)

Relations with the Legislature

1. In general, how did you conduct your contacts with the legislature? (Establish degree of access and courtesy with which received. Determine the existence of a formal lobbying network; special efforts directed toward legislators in leadership positions; the use of headcounts, district contacts, or electoral threats; and main arguments used.)

2. Who else helped you in influencing the legislature? (Establish the position and level of activity of female legislators, political parties, the governor and other elected officials, state Commission on the Status of Women, and the general public. Determine if endorsements from state and community leaders were sought and with what results. Try to establish some basis for comparison with other issues concerning state and community leaders' activism on the ERA. Determine if grass-roots education was attempted, with speakers bureaus and literature. Ask for copies of printed strategies and other literature used.)

3. How has the ERA developed as an issue? (Determine the existence and direction of any changing sentiment toward the ERA in the legislature and among groups and the general public. Determine changes in the levels of activity over time of proponent and opposition groups.)

4. How do you evaluate the campaign? What do you think your side should have done differently? (Establish respondent's perception of the most effective tactics.)

Legislative Action

1. Who were the legislative sponsors for the ERA? (Determine if groups played a role in selecting the sponsors and any cosponsors. Establish the nature of the group's relationship with the sponsors after introduction.)

2. Tell me about the hearings on the ERA. (Establish if hearings must be held; the role groups played in their scheduling; length; supporter-opponent ratio among witnesses and the audience; and

identity and residence of witnesses. Determine any other role groups played in committee deliberations such as providing reference material or assistance in writing the report.)

3. How is the legislature divided on the ERA? (Determine if there seems to be a partisan division or cleavages along urban-rural, regional, racial, or ideological lines.)

4. What arguments concerning the ERA seem to be most effective with legislators supporting the ERA? What about those who oppose the ERA?

5. What actions have the legislature taken on the ERA?

The Opposition

1. How and when did you first become aware of strong opposition to (support for) the ERA? (Establish the identification and number of such groups; the dominant group; and the past political experience, community prominence, and educational-occupational status of their leadership and membership.)

2. What types of tactics have these groups and individuals used? (Establish the methods used in dealing with the opposition.)

3. (Texas only.) Have there been any moves to rescind ratification? (Determine the nature of this movement, its leadership, and legislative responses. Determine the proponents' response to the rescission movement.)

Media Coverage

1. What is your opinion of the media's coverage of the ERA?

2. In what ways did you or your group use the media in the ERA campaign? (Determine if these tactics were used: paid ads, meetings with the media, letters to the editor, press releases and press conferences, TV/radio panel and talk show appearances.)

Appendix C

Interview Guide for Legislators Actively Involved in Equal Rights Amendment Ratification

Introduction to the ERA

1. In comparison with other issues coming before the legislature, how did the ERA rank in terms of interest groups involved? (Also establish relative public, media, and legislative involvement.)

2. When you first heard about the ERA, what was your attitude toward it? (Establish the approximate date and any changes in attitude subsequently.)

3. Over time, did those groups supporting it become more active? What about the opposition?

4. Has there been any change in support for the ERA in the legislature over time? In what direction?

5. How is the legislature divided on the ERA? (Determine if there seems to be a partisan division, cleavages along urban-rural, regional, racial, or ideological lines, or unusual influence by a particular interest group.)

6. Which arguments concerning the ERA seem to be used most often by legislators like you? What about those who disagree with you on the ERA?

Group Involvement on the ERA

1. Whom did you hear from concerning the ERA? (Determine if contacts from groups, the governor, the general public, other legislators, other elected or appointed officials, or media were recalled. Determine if these people were previously known to the legislator.)

2. In general, how did interested persons attempt to influence legislators like you? (Determine if the following tactics were used: demonstrations, petitions, letter-writing, headcounts, district contacts, threat of electoral sanctions. Determine main arguments used by groups.)

3. Did some groups seem to be more effective than others in influencing legislators like you? (Establish any negative attitudes directed toward certain groups; whom he/she felt the various groups "represented"; and the most effective group tactics.)

For Sponsor Only

1. How did you come to sponsor the ERA? (Establish any role of groups in recruitment of sponsor and the relationship between proponents and the sponsor.)

2. Beyond introducing the resolution, did you try to build support for the ERA in the legislature?

For Female Legislators Only

1. As a woman, did you feel it necessary to take a leadership role on the ERA resolution?

2. Did you try to build support for (opposition to) the ERA? (Determine whether respondent tried to influence other legislators and his/her participation in hearings and floor debate.)

Legislative Action

1. Tell me about the hearings on the ERA. (Establish if hearings must be held; the role groups played in their scheduling; length; supporter-opponent ratio among witnesses and the audience; and the impact of the hearings upon legislators. Determine any other role groups played in committee deliberations such as providing reference material or assistance in writing the report.)

2. What actions has the legislature taken on the ERA? (Include committee actions.)

3. Was there a full floor debate on the ERA? (Establish length; number and issue stance of speakers; and role of groups in recruiting speakers.)

4. (Texas only.) Has the legislature considered rescinding the ERA? (Determine legislative support for rescission; legislative leadership; group involvement; and legislative action.)

Appendix D

Organizations Supporting the Equal Rights Amendment, 1972

Women's Organizations

American Association of University Women (AAUW)
American Federation of Soroptomists
American Home Economics Association
American Medical Women's Association, Inc.
American Nurses Association
American Society of Women Accountants
American Society of Women Certified Public Accountants
American Women in Radio and Television
Association of American Women Dentists
Association of American Women in Science
B'nai B'rith Women
Federally Employed Women (FEW)
Federation of Women Shareholders in American Business, Inc.
General Federation of Women's Clubs (GFWC)
Intercollegiate Association of Women Students
Interstate Association of Commissions on the Status of Women
Ladies Auxiliary of V.F.W. of the United States
Ladies of the Grand Army of the Republic
League for American Working Women (LAWN)
League of Women Voters (LWV)
National Association of Colored Women's Clubs
National Association of Negro Business and Professional Women's
  Clubs
National Association of Women Deans, Administrators and
  Counselors

National Association of Women Lawyers
National Council of Women Chiropractors
National Council of Women of the United States
National Federation of Business and Professional Women's Clubs, Inc. (BPW)
National Federation of Republican Women's Clubs (NFRWC)
National Organization for Women (NOW)
National Secretaries Association
National Woman's Party (NWP)
National Women's Political Caucus (NWPC)
Order of Women Legislators
Professional Women's Caucus
Women's Christian Temperance Union (WCTU)
Women's Equity Action League (WEAL)
Women's International League for Peace and Freedom (WILPF)
Women's Joint Legislative Committee for Equal Rights
Women's Liberation
Women United
Young Women's Christian Association (YWCA)
Zonta International

Church Organizations

American Association of Women Ministers
American Jewish Congress
Church Women United
Council for Christian Social Action, United Church of Christ
Ecumenical Task Force on Women and Religion (Catholic Caucus)
National Board of the Leadership Conference of Women Religious
National Coalition of American Nuns
National Council of Jewish Women
Network
St. Joan's International Alliance of Catholic Women, United States Section
Unitarian Universalist Association
Unitarian Universalist Women's Federation
United Methodist Church—Women's Division
United Presbyterian Church
United Presbyterian Women
Women Theologians United (Catholic Caucus)

Women's Committee on Freedom in the Church, National
  Association of Laymen (Catholic)

Labor Organizations

American Federation of State, County, and Municipal Employees
  (AFSCME)
American Federation of Teachers (Affiliate of the AFL–CIO)
American Newspaper Guild
Communications Workers of America (AFL–CIO)
International Brotherhood of Painters and Allied Trades
International Brotherhood of Teamsters
International Chemical Workers Union
International Union of Electrical, Radio and Machine Workers
  (AFL–CIO)
International Union of United Automobile, Aerospace, and
  Agricultural Implement Workers of America (UAW)
National Association of Railway Business Women, Inc.
United Farm Workers (UFW)
United Steelworkers of America (AFL–CIO)

Other Organizations

American Association of College Deans
American Bar Association (ABA)
American Civil Liberties Union (ACLU)
Americans for Democratic Action (ADA)
American Psychological Association
American Public Health Association
American Society of Microbiology
American Veterans Committee
Association of the Bar of the City of New York
Citizens' Advisory Council on the Status of Women
Common Cause
Council for Women's Rights
Democratic Party
International Association of Human Rights Agencies
Men's League for Women's Rights
National Ad Hoc Committee for the Passage of Equal Rights
  Amendment

National Association for the Advancement of Colored People (NAACP)

National Association of College Deans, Registrars, and Administrative Officers

National Education Association (NEA)

National Grange

National Welfare Rights Organization (NWRO)

President's Task Force on Women's Rights and Responsibilities

Republican Party

Theta Sigma Phi

U.S. Civil Rights Commission

U.S. Department of Labor and the Women's Bureau

Zero Population Growth (ZPG)

SOURCE: Citizens' Advisory Council on the Status of Women and the American Association of University Women.

Appendix E

Organizations on Record in Opposition to the Equal Rights Amendment

American Conservative Union (ACU)
American Independent Party (AIP)
American Legion (Minn.)
American Party (AP)
American Women Against Ratification of ERA (AWARE)
American Women Already Richly Endowed (AWARE)*
Arkansas Women Against the ERA
Christian Crusade
Citizens Against ERA (Ohio)
Citizens Against the Draft (Fla.)
Citizens Organized for the Protection in Education of Children (Ohio)
Committee for Retention and Protection of Women's Rights (Miss.)*
Committee to Expose the Equal Rights Amendment (Ind.)**
Committee to Preserve Women's Rights (CPWR, Tex.)
Committee to Repeal the ERA (Tex.)
Communist Party, U.S.A.
Concerned Parents Committee (Wis.)
Congress of Freedom
Daughters of the American Revolution (DAR)
Daughters of the Colonial Wars (Va.)
Equal Rights Amendment Steering Endeavor (ERASE, Ind.)
Farm Bureau (Va.)
Federation of Republican Women's Clubs (Ala., Conn., Fla.)
Females Opposed to Equality (FOE)
Feminine Anti-Feminists (Ohio)

General Federation of Women's Clubs (Va., Ill.)
Gi Gi Gals Galore Against the ERA (Fla.)
Grandmothers United Against the ERA (Ohio)
Happiness of Motherhood Eternal (HOME)
Happiness of Womanhood (HOW)
Home Administrators, Inc. (HA!)
Homemakers' United Efforts (HUE, Ariz.)
Housewives and Motherhood Anti-Lib Movement (HAM, Ohio)
Humanitarians Opposed to Degrading Our Girls (HOTDOG, Utah)**
International Anti-Women's Liberation League (IAWLL)
Iowa Women Against the ERA
John Birch Society
Ku Klux Klan (KKK)
Leadership Foundation
League for the Protection of Women and Children (Mo.)*
League of Housewives***
League of Large Families
Liberty Lobby
Minnesota T (Taxpayer) Party
Minnesotians Against the ERA
Montana Citizens to Rescind the ERA
National Coalition for Accountability
National Committee of Endorsers Against ERA*
National Council of Catholic Laity (NCCL)
National Council of Catholic Women (NCCW)
National States Rights Party
Parents of New York United
People Leadership (Fla.)
Pro America
Protect Our Women (POW, Wis.)**
Rabbinical Alliance of America
Rabbinical Society of America
Repeal ERA (Neb.)
Restore Our American Republic (ROAR, Ohio)
Revolutionary Union (Wis.)
Right to Life (Minn., Kan.)
Right to Be a Woman (Ill.)
Scratch Women's Lib (Conn., Ind.)*
Society for the Christian Commonwealth
Stop ERA

Union Women's Alliance to Gain Equality (Union WAGE, Cal.)
United Conservatives of Indiana
Viva La Difference Committee
We the People**
Winsome Wives and Homemakers (Wis.)
Wisconsin Legislative and Research Committee, Inc.
Women Against the Draft (Fla.)
Women for Constitutional Government
Women for Maintaining the Differences Between the Sexes and
     Against the ERA (Wy.)**
Women for Responsible Legislation
Women of Industry
Women Opposed to ERA (WOE, Kansas)
Women United to Defend Existing Rights (WUNDER, N.Y.)
Women Who Want to Be Women (WWWW)
Women's Committee to Rescind the ERA (Ky.)
Women's Freedom Fund (N.Y.)
Wyoming Women for Privacy and Against the ERA**
Young Americans for Freedom (YAF)

   *Organizations affiliated with Stop ERA or were founded by Phyl-
   lis Schlafly.
  **Organizations which have John Birch Society origins.
***Organizations affiliated with Happiness of Womanhood.

SOURCE: Newspaper stories and personal interviews.

Bibliography

Books

Almond, Gabriel, and Verba, Sidney. *The Civic Culture.* Boston: Little, Brown, 1965.

Bachrach, Peter, and Baratz, Morton S. *Power and Poverty.* New York: Oxford University Press, 1970.

Bauer, Raymond A., et al. *American Business and Public Policy.* New York: Atherton, 1963.

Bentley, Arthur A. *The Process of Government.* Bloomington, Ind.: Principia, 1949.

Brown, Barbara, et al. *Women's Rights and the Law: The Impact of the ERA on State Laws.* New York: Praeger, 1977.

Burdick, Eugene, and Brodbeck, Arthur J., eds. *American Voting Behavior.* Glencoe, Ill.: Free Press, 1959.

California Commission on the Status of Women. *Impact ERA: Limitations and Possibilities.* Millbrae, Cal.: Les Femmes, 1976.

Carden, Maren Lockwood. *The New Feminist Movement.* New York: Russell Sage Foundation, 1974.

Chafe, William H. *The American Woman: Her Changing Social, Economic, and Political Role, 1920–1970.* New York: Oxford University Press, 1972.

Clapp, Charles L. *The Congressman: His Work as He Sees it.* Garden City, N.Y.: Doubleday, 1963.

Clausen, Aage R. *How Congressmen Decide: A Policy Focus.* New York: St. Martin's, 1973.

Cobb, Roger W., and Elder, Charles D. *Participation in American Politics: The Dynamics of Agenda-Building.* Boston: Allyn & Bacon, 1972.

Coleman, James S. *Community Conflict*. New York: Free Press, 1957.

Crain, Robert L., et al. *The Politics of Community Conflict: The Fluoridation Decision*. Indianapolis: Bobbs-Merrill, 1969.

Davison, Jaquie. *I Am a Housewife*. New York: Guild, 1972.

DeCrow, Karen. *Sexist Justice*. New York: Random House, 1974.

Edelman, Murray. *The Symbolic Uses of Politics*. Urbana: University of Illinois Press, 1964.

Francis, Wayne L. *Legislative Issues in the Fifty States: A Comparative Analysis*. Chicago: Rand McNally, 1967.

Freeman, Jo. *The Politics of Women's Liberation*. New York: Longman, 1975.

The Gallup Poll: Public Opinion, 1935–1971. New York: Random House, 1972.

Gamson, William A. *The Strategy of Social Protest*. Homewood, Ill.: Dorsey, 1975.

Gornick, Vivian, and Moran, Barbara K., eds. *Woman in Sexist Society*. New York: New American Library, 1972.

Gouldner, Alvin W., ed. *Studies in Leadership: Leadership and Democratic Action*. New York: Harper & Row, 1950.

Gruberg, Martin. *Women in American Politics: An Assessment and Sourcebook*. Oshkosh, Wis.: Academic, 1968.

Gusfield, Joseph R., ed. *Protest, Reform, and Revolt: A Reader in Social Movements*. New York: Wiley, 1970.

Hall, Donald R. *Cooperative Lobbying—The Power of Pressure*. Tuscon: University of Arizona Press, 1969.

Harris, Louis, and Associates. *The 1972 Virginia Slims American Women's Opinion Poll*. New York, 1972.

Hole, Judith, and Levine, Ellen. *Rebirth of Feminism*. New York: Quadrangle, 1971.

Kanowitz, Leo. *Sex Roles in Law and Society: Cases and Materials*. Albuquerque: University of New Mexico Press, 1972.

Kanowitz, Leo. *Women and the Law: The Unfinished Revolution*. Albuquerque: University of New Mexico Press, 1969.

Kenney, David. *Basic Illinois Government: A Systematic Explanation*. Carbondale: Southern Illinois University Press, 1970.

Key, V. O., Jr. *Politics, Parties, and Pressure Groups*. 5th ed. New York: Crowell, 1964.

Kingdon, John W. *Congressmen's Voting Decisions*. New York: Harper & Row, 1973.

Kirkpatrick, Jeane J. *Political Woman*. New York: Basic, 1974.

Matthews, Donald R. *U.S. Senators and Their World*. New York: Vintage, 1960.

McCourt, Kathleen. *Working-Class Women and Grass-Roots Politics*. Bloomington: University of Indiana Press, 1977.

Milbrath, Lester. *The Washington Lobbyists*. Chicago: Rand McNally, 1963.

Murphy, Irene L. *Public Policy on the Status of Women*. Lexington, Mass.: Heath, 1973.

Myrdal, Gunnar. *An American Dilemma*. New York: Harper & Row, 1944.

Platt, Anthony M., ed. *Politics of Riot Commissions*. New York: Macmillan, 1971.

Presthus, Robert. *Elites in the Policy Process*. New York: Cambridge University Press, 1974.

The Roper Organization, Inc. *The Virginia Slims American Women's Opinion Poll*. New York, 1974.

Ross, Susan C. *The Rights of Women*. New York: Avon, 1973.

Schattschneider, E. E. *The Semi-Sovereign People*. New York: Holt, Rinehart and Winston, 1960.

Seifer, Nancy. *Absent from the Majority: Working Class Women in America*. New York: American Jewish Committee National Project on Ethnic America, 1973.

Steiner, Gilbert Y., and Gove, Samuel K. *Legislative Politics in Illinois*. Urbana: University of Illinois Press, 1960.

Truman, David. *The Governmental Process*. New York: Knopf, 1951.

Wootten, Graham. *Interest-Groups*. Englewood Cliffs, N.J.: Prentice-Hall, 1970.

Zeigler, Harmon, and Baer, Michael. *Lobbying: Interaction and Influence in American State Legislatures*. Belmont, Cal.: Wadsworth, 1969.

Articles

Arnott, Catherine. "Feminists and Anti-Feminists as 'True Believers.'" *Sociology and Social Research* 57 (April 1973): 300–306.

Beeman, Alice L., and McCune, Shirley. "Changing Styles: Women's Groups in the Seventies." *AAUW Journal* 64 (November 1970): 24–26.

Black, Gordon S. "Conflict in the Community: A Theory of the Effects of Community Size." *American Political Science Review* 68 (September 1974): 1245–61.

Blitz, Rudolf. "Women in the Professions." *Monthly Labor Review* 97 (May 1974): 34–39.

Bonilla, Frank. "When Is Petition 'Pressure'?" *Public Opinion Quarterly* 20 (Spring 1956): 39–48.

Brady, David W., and Tedin, Kent L. "Ladies in Pink: Religion and

Political Ideology in the Anti-ERA Movement." *Social Science Quarterly* 56 (March 1976): 564–75.

Crain, Robert L., and Rosenthal, Donald B. "Community Status as a Dimension of Local Decision-Making." *American Sociological Review* 32 (December 1967): 970–84.

Crane, Wilder, Jr. "Test of Effectiveness of Interest-Group Pressure on Legislators." *Southwest Social Science Quarterly* 41 (December 1960):335–40.

Emerson, Thomas I., et al. "The Equal Rights Amendment: A Constitutional Basis for Equal Rights for Women." *Yale Law Journal* 80 (April 1971): 871–985.

Freund, Paul. "The Equal Rights Amendment Is Not the Way." *Harvard Civil Rights–Civil Liberties Law Review* 6 (March 1971): 234–42.

Gamson, William A. "Rancorous Conflict in Community Politics." *American Sociological Review* 31 (February 1966): 71–81.

Garceau, Oliver, and Silverman, Corinne. "A Pressure Group and the Pressured: A Case Report." *American Political Science Review* 48 (September 1954): 672–91.

Hacker, Helen Mayer. "Women as a Minority Group." *Social Forces* 30 (October 1951): 60–69.

Heckman, J. William, Jr. "Ratification of a Constitutional Amendment: Can a State Change Its Mind?" *Connecticut Law Review* 6 (1973): 28–35.

Joyner, Nancy D. "The Commonwealth's Approach to the Equal Rights Amendment." *University of Virginia Newsletter* 50 (15 May, 1974): 33–36.

Kirby, David J., and Crain, Robert L. "Functions of Conflict: School Desegregation in 91 Cities." *Social Science Quarterly* 55 (September 1974): 478–92.

Longley, Lawrence D. "Interest Group Interactions in a Legislative System." *Journal of Politics* 29 (August 1967): 637–58.

Mack, Raymond W., and Snyder, Richard C. "The Analysis of Social Conflict: Toward an Overview and Synthesis." *Journal of Conflict Resolution* 1 (June 1957): 212–48.

March, James G. "Husband-Wife Interaction over Political Issues." *Public Opinion Quarterly* 17 (Winter 1953–54): 461–70.

Morris, Monica B. "Newspapers and the New Feminists: Black Out as Social Control?" *Journalism Quarterly* 50 (Spring 1973): 37–42.

Morris, Monica B. "Public Definition of a Social Movement: Women's Liberation." *Sociology and Social Research* 57 (July 1973): 526–43.

Planell, Raymond M. "The Equal Rights Amendment: Will States Be Allowed to Change Their Minds?" *Notre Dame Lawyer* 49 (February 1974) 657–70.

Rose, Arnold M. "Voluntary Associations under Conditions of Competition and Conflict." *Social Forces* 34 (December 1955): 159–63.

Safran, Claire. "What You Should Know about the Equal Rights Amendment." *Redbook* 141 (June 1973): 62ff.

Schmitz, John G. "Look Out: They're Planning to Draft Your Daughter." *American Opinion* 15 (November 1972): 1–16.

Stoloff, Carolyn. "Who Joins Women's Liberation?" *Psychiatry* 36 (August 1973): 325–40.

Sussman, Leila. "Mass Political Letter Writing in America: The Growth of an Institution." *Public Opinion Quarterly* 23 (Summer 1959): 205–12.

Tavris, Carol, and Jayaratne, Toby. "What 120,000 Young Women Can Tell You about Sex, Motherhood, Menstruation, Housework—and Men," *Redbook* 140 (January 1973): 67ff.

Wohl, Lisa Cronin, "Phyllis Schlafly: The Sweetheart of the Silent Majority," *Ms.* 2 (March 1974): 55–57ff.

Wohl, Lisa Cronin. "White Gloves and Combat Boots: The Fight for ERA," *Civil Liberties Review* 1 (Fall 1974): 77–86.

Wright, Charles R., and Hyman, Herbert H. "Voluntary Association Memberships of American Adults: Evidence from National Sample Surveys," *American Sociological Review* 23 (June 1958): 284–94.

Zeigler, Harmon, and Baer, Michael A. "The Recruitment of Lobbyists and Legislators," *Midwest Journal of Political Science* 12 (November 1968): 493–513.

Documents

U.S. Citizens' Advisory Council on the Status of Women. *The Equal Rights Amendment–Senator Ervin's Minority Report and the Yale Law Journal.* Washington, D.C.: Government Printing Office, 1972.

U.S. Citizens' Advisory Council on the Status of Women. *Interpretation of the Equal Rights Amendment in Accordance with Legislative History.* Washington, D.C.: Government Printing Office, 1974.

U.S. Congress. Senate. Committee on the Judiciary. *Equal Rights,*

1970: Hearings on S.J. Res. 61 and S.J. Res. 231, 91st Cong., 2d
sess., 1970, pp. 9–150.

U.S. Congress. Senate. Committee on the Judiciary. *Equal Rights for
Men and Women: Report to Accompany S.J. Res. 8, S.J. Res. 9, and
H.J. Res. 208*. 92nd Cong., 2d sess., 1972, S. Rept. 689.

U.S. Congress. House. *Congressional Record*. 92nd Cong., 1st sess.,
1972, 117, pt. 27.

U.S. Congress. Senate. *Congressional Record* 92d Cong., 2d sess.,
1972, 118, pt. 3.

U.S. Congress. Senate. *Congressional Record*, 92d Cong., 2d sess.,
1972, 118, pt. 7.

U.S. Department of Commerce Census Bureau. *Current Population
Report* (1976), Bulletin P-60, no. 101.

U.S. Department of Labor. Women's Bureau. *The Earnings Gap Between Women and Men*. Washington, D.C.: Government Printing
Office, 1976.

U.S. Department of Labor. Women's Bureau. *1969 Handbook on
Women Workers*. Washington, D.C.: Government Printing Office,
1969.

U.S. Department of Labor. Women's Bureau. *1975 Handbook on
Women Workers*. Washington, D.C.: Government Printing Office,
1975.

U.S. Department of Labor. Women's Bureau. *Women Workers Today*.
Washington, D.C.: Government Printing Office, 1976.

U.S. National Center for Education Statistics. *Earned Degrees Conferred 1974–75*. Washington, D.C.: Government Printing Office,
1977.

Index